ASSERTIVENESS AT WORK

A practical guide to handling awkward situations
Second Edition

ASSERTIVENESS AT WORK

A practical guide to handling awkward situations
Second Edition

Ken Back and Kate Back with Terry Bates

McGRAW-HILL BOOK COMPANY

London · New York · St Louis · San Francisco · Auckland · Bogotá
Caracas · Hamburg · Lisbon · Madrid · Mexico · Milan
Montreal · New Delhi · Panama · Paris · San Juan · São Paulo
Singapore · Sydney · Tokyo · Toronto

Published by
McGRAW-HILL Book Company Europe
Shoppenhangers Road, Maidenhead, Berkshire, SL6 2QL, England
Telephone 0628 23432
Fax 0628 770224

British Library Cataloguing in Publication Data

Back, Ken
    Assertiveness at work: a practical guide to handling awkward situations. – 2nd ed.
    1. Interpersonal relationships. Communication. Assertive behaviour
    I. Title   II. Back, Kate   III. Bates, Terry
    158.2
    ISBN 0–07–707377–0
    ISBN 0–07–707378–9 pbk

Library of Congress Cataloging-in-Publication Data

Back, Ken.
    Assertiveness at work: a practical guide to handling awkward situations/Ken and Kate
Back with Terry Bates. – 2nd ed.
       p.   cm.
    Includes index.
    ISBN 0–07–707377–0 (hardback) – ISBN 0–07–707378–9 (paperback)
    1. Communication in personnel management. 2. Assertiveness (Psychology). 3. Inter-
personal relations. 4. Management-Psychological aspects.
    I. Back, Kate. II. Bates, Terry. III. Title.
    HF5549.5.C6B23 1990
    658.4'092–dc20

   345CUP9432

Typeset by Computape (Pickering) Ltd, North Yorkshire
Printed and bound in Great Britain at the University Press, Cambridge.

Contents

The Authors

Ken and Kate Back are the founders and directors of Context Training Ltd., which specializes in assertiveness training for people at work. In this practical book, Ken and Kate have brought together their experience in training thousands of people to be more assertive. In addition to books, they have written numerous articles, advised on and produced videos, and appeared on television programmes about assertiveness. They have made a significant contribution to the development and spread of assertiveness training.

Terry Bates, a psychologist in management and organizational development, has worked extensively in both educational and commercial organizations. He now specializes in counselling executives in assertiveness for personal and organizational change.

INFORMATION ON CONTEXT TRAINING

Ken and Kate Back can be contacted at:

Context Training Ltd.
PO Box 33
Henley-on-Thames
Oxon
RG9 1YN

Tel: 0491 411341

Preface

If you have to deal with other people as part of your job, then this book is meant for you. It does not matter whether you work for a large company, a public corporation, a medium-sized family business, or a one-man or woman concern—just as long as your work brings you into contact with other people. So whatever your job—whether you manage a number of people or are a specialist advising and influencing others—this book will be useful to you.

It is likely that in the course of your work you will face a number of tricky situations from time to time. For instance, have you ever experienced any of the following?

- Being faced with unreasonable requests from your manager
- Feeling angry about the cooperation you are getting from another department
- Having to convey a decision that you know your staff will not like
- Wanting to disagree with a point of view that a senior manager is forcefully expressing
- Having to handle an irate customer without losing his or her valuable business or making promises that are difficult to keep
- Making an important presentation to a group of senior managers having had very little time to prepare

We call these situations 'tricky' because they often make you feel uncomfortable, anxious, angry, or frustrated and they can sometimes lead to open conflict. Any of these things can happen when your needs, wants, beliefs or opinions are *different* from the needs, wants, beliefs, or opinions of the other people involved. These situations, and many like them, occur in all organizations. We believe that your success at work, and thus the success of your organization, can be affected by the way you handle these situations. We say this because *the outcome of any situation can be very different according to how it is handled.*

This book is about handling these and many other situations in a way that is mutually acceptable to all parties concerned. From our own personal experiences and from working with managers we have concluded that this usually means behaving *assertively*, as opposed to *nonassertively* or *aggressively*.

So the book focuses on the *behaviour* you can use when handling various situations. The word 'behaviour' can be used to refer to a whole range of observable activities in which people engage. But we mostly use it in a particular way—to refer to *the things you do and say* when you are communicating with other people. The book also looks at what lies behind the behaviour, not in terms of general aspects of personality, but in terms of the specific beliefs, thoughts, and feelings you may have that affect the behaviour you use. We concentrate on behaviour, beliefs, thoughts, and feelings because, as we hope to demonstrate in the book, they can be changed!

Of course, it is not easy to change these things, but it can be done. With practice you can change your beliefs, thoughts, behaviour, and even your feelings, especially if you tackle them in small steps, concentrating on one, at most two, specific aspects at a time. This brings us to say something about how to use the book. If you want to get maximum mileage out of it, then we suggest you dip into the book a chunk at a time. What we had in mind when we arranged Chapters 1–7 was that you would probably want to get to grips with the preliminary concepts and then do some practice before digging further into the concepts. Chapters 8–10 are slightly different, in that they help you not only to handle tricky situations, but in particular to handle the people whose own aggressive or nonassertive behaviour makes a situation even more difficult. In Chapters 11–14 we look at applications of assertiveness. Then in Chapter 15 we give some practical suggestions on how you can continue to be more assertive after you have finished reading this book.

This book presents a third option in the area of behaviour: assertiveness. It gets you to focus on *yourself*, what *you can do*, and moves you away from being at the mercy of other people's behaviour and the adverse effects this can have on you. Not only will assertiveness help you to become more effective in your job, but it will also lead to greater personal satisfaction in your dealings with other people.

This new edition comes from our experiences in assertion training over the past ten years. Many people have helped us to learn from these experiences, in particular our associates with whom we work closely:

Paul Whiteby who did much of the original work on stress

Sue Knight for her fresh insights on beliefs

Conrad Potts for his challenging ideas on win/win

Terry Bates who has contributed the chapters on change and stress

So our thanks to them, and to the thousands of individual managers and specialists who have attended our training courses and who have constantly provoked us to new thinking and new possibilities.

We would like to thank our friend, Liz Banfield, who patiently waded through our original (and sometimes almost illegible) manuscript to produce a first class typescript for us. Not only that but she willingly repeated the exercise for us for this new edition.

Ken Back and Kate Back
April 1990

1. Assertion, nonassertion and aggression

The word 'assertion' appeals to us because it is a familiar word rather than a new bit of jargon. The dictionary defines it in two ways: an affirmation, a declaration, or a positive statement; insistence upon a right. Unfortunately, though, in common usage the word often refers to behaviour that *we* would call aggression. These different uses can be confusing. So let us begin this chapter by clarifying the way we use the terms 'assertion', 'nonassertion', and 'aggression' to refer to three types of behaviour. We will then examine the different effects of the three behaviours and look at how people come to behave nonassertively and aggressively, ending the chapter with some general considerations about assertiveness.

What we mean by 'assertion'

We use the word 'assertion' (or the abbreviation 'ass') to refer to behaviour that involves:

- Standing up for your own rights in such a way that you do not violate another person's rights
- Expressing your needs, wants, opinions, feelings and beliefs in direct, honest and appropriate ways

We will demonstrate this with an example. Suppose your manager asked you to complete some additional work by the end of the month. You are the best person to do the work, but your time is already fully committed to other work. An assertive response in this situation could be:
'I appreciate that you would like this work completed by the end of the month. However, I don't see that I can fit it in with our workload as it is at present.'
So assertiveness is based on the *beliefs* that in any situation:

- You have needs to be met
- The other people involved have needs to be met
- You have rights; so do others
- You have something to contribute; so do others

The aim of assertive behaviour is to satisfy the needs and wants of both parties involved in the situation.

1

What we mean by 'nonassertion'

We use the words 'nonassertion' (or 'na') to refer to behaviour when it involves the following:

- Failing to stand up for your rights or doing so in such a way that others can easily disregard them
- Expressing your needs, wants, opinions, feelings, and beliefs in apologetic, diffident, or self-effacing ways
- Failing to express honestly your needs, wants, opinions, feelings, and beliefs

So, if we return to the previous situation, a nonassertive response could be: 'Well, I don't really have any spare time, but I suppose I could work late to fit the extra work in, er ... I don't mind.'
Nonassertion is based upon the *beliefs* that in any situation:

- The other person's needs and wants are more important than your own
- The other person has rights, but you do not
- You have little or nothing to contribute; the other person has a great deal to contribute

The aim of nonassertion is to avoid conflict and to please others.

What we mean by 'aggression'

We use the word 'aggression' ('agg') to refer to behaviour that consists of the following:

- Standing up for your own rights, but doing so in such a way that you violate the rights of other people
- Ignoring or dismissing the needs, wants, opinions, feelings, or beliefs of others
- Expressing your own needs, wants, and opinions (which may be honest or dishonest) in inappropriate ways

An aggressive response to the example situation could be:
'What! I'm up to my eyes in work already. There's no way I can do that.'
Aggressive behaviour is based on the *belief* that:

- Your own needs, wants, and opinions are more important than other people's
- You have rights but other people do not
- You have something to contribute; others have little or nothing to contribute

2

The aim of aggression is to win, if necessary at the expense of others.

So these are the three basic types of behaviour that all of us can use. Below is another example illustrating the three different behaviours being used to handle the same situation.

Situation	*Taking an unsatisfactory letter back to the person who has produced it*
Assertion	'Jane, I'd like you to re-do this letter as there are several mistakes in it.'
Nonassertion	You find an excuse not to take the letter back, or you say: 'I know it's, um ... probably my fault in ... not writing very clearly, but is there, um ... any chance at all you could find a spare minute to um ... just change one or two small things on this letter for me.'
Aggression	'I don't know how you've got the nerve to give me this sort of stuff for signing. It's full of mistakes.'

A WORD ABOUT 'RIGHTS'

In defining the three different types of behaviour, we have referred several times to 'rights'. We go into detail on this in Chapter 3, but for the moment let us say that a right is *something to which you are entitled.* In any situation, you will have rights; other people will have rights. Thus, in the situation above, you have the right to expect and receive a letter of the standard agreed (assuming this *has* been agreed). You have the right to point out mistakes to the person who has produced it. The other person has the right to have these mistakes pointed out in a reasonable manner, so that they are not personally under attack or made to look small. Unless you are clear on the rights in a situation, you cannot know whether you are being assertive.

We will now examine the effects of nonassertion and aggression and then look at how these behaviours come about.

The effects of nonassertion

As we have said, when you behave nonassertively you are aiming to avoid conflict and to please others. But in pursuing this aim, your nonassertion has effects: on the outcome of the situation, on yourself, on other people, and on your organization. Let us look at each of these in turn.

EFFECTS ON THE OUTCOME OF THE SITUATION

Let us return to the first situation we described. Just to recap, your manager has asked you to complete some new work by the end of the month. You are the best person to do the work, but you have no spare time available. A nonassertive response was: 'Well, I don't really have any spare time but I

3

suppose I could work late to fit the extra work in, er ... I don't mind.' The outcome in this situation, as a result of that particular nonassertion, is likely to be that you would agree to take on more work than you could handle in normal working hours. We would not regard this as a satisfactory outcome because it does not meet the needs *of both parties*. True, in some instances you may get what you want. All too often, though, the other person gets what they want. Either way, these are not outcomes that meet both sets of needs. In addition, in many situations your nonassertion will lead to *low-quality* outcomes—an impractical solution, a weak compromise, an unclear or belated decision, and so on.

EFFECTS ON YOU

Short-term effects
Immediately after a nonassertion like the response in the previous example, it is likely that you would experience a number of effects. We cannot say precisely what these would be because we cannot observe them, but they might be any of the following:

- A reduction in anxiety because you have avoided a potential conflict with your manager
- An escape from feelings of guilt, which would have followed from upsetting your manager by saying 'No' to him or her
- Feeling sorry for yourself because you are the 'poor soul who gets landed with all the work'
- A feeling of pride that you take on so much work

We refer to these effects as short-term consequences, because they follow immediately after a behaviour. These immediate consequences and other similar ones are usually pleasant for you (strangely enough, you can even enjoy feeling sorry for yourself) and thus they reinforce your nonassertion. By this, we mean *they increase the chances that you will behave nonassertively again*. Let us illustrate this with an example.

Tomorrow you know you have a difficult situation to handle when you have to tell Mike, a member of your staff, that he has not been given the regrading of his job that he was expecting. You know he is going to be annoyed and will probably start blaming you for not pushing hard enough. Thinking about this makes you feel anxious and tense. When you get into work in the morning you find that Mike has phoned in to say he is sick and will not be in today. Immediately you feel a reduction in tension ('Phew! Thank goodness I shan't have to face that today'). Because this is a pleasant experience you will look for ways to repeat it. So tomorrow when Mike is in, you find an excuse not to face up to him (perhaps you are too busy in meetings). This pattern is repeated the day after, so that you are putting off facing up to a difficult situation. Your nonassertion is being reinforced.

Reinforcement can also come from other people. For instance, colleagues may say things like: 'That's very good, you're always willing to stay late', or 'You don't mind putting yourself out', or 'You never upset anyone, you don't rock the boat'. These help to reinforce your nonassertion.

While the immediate consequences of nonassertion are pleasant, the longer-term ones can be unpleasant and undesirable for yourself, for others and for the organization you work for.

Longer-term effects
Frequent nonassertion will result in your experiencing a growing loss of self-esteem. Self-esteem is the valuation you hold about yourself as a person. (There is further explanation of this concept towards the end of this chapter.)

This comes about as you recognize that you are unable to take initiatives, or to face up to difficult situations (like the example above about a member of staff's job regrading). This may lead to you being angry or frustrated with yourself, feeling hurt or dropping into sustained self-pity. These feelings are directed inwards at yourself, and lead to increased internal tensions, which in turn make it more difficult for you to behave assertively. Unless these internal tensions are released they may also lead to increased occurrences of psychosomatic problems, like headaches, backaches, and so on.

So the pattern looks like this:

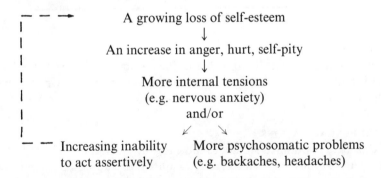

There can also be 'loop back' within this pattern at various points.

These longer-term consequences are obviously undesirable, but in spite of this, nonassertion *continues* if reinforced by short-term effects.

EFFECTS OF NONASSERTION ON OTHERS
Initially other people feel sorry for you when you behave nonassertively: sorry that you find yourself in situations you find difficult to handle, sorry that you do not have the skills to speak up for yourself. Following on from

this, some people may feel guilty if they think they are taking advantage of your nonassertion. For example, they may feel guilty about making a request of you when they know you are unable to say 'No' even though you might want to. Other people might feel indifferent about you in these circumstances. After a while, people start feeling irritated by your repeated nonassertion, saying such things as: 'For heaven's sake, why don't you say what you want?' or 'Why didn't you say so at the time rather than when it's too late?'

Continued nonassertion ultimately leads others to have a lack of respect for you. This is because they do not know what you stand for, or because they doubt your integrity, believing that you will say one thing but go away and do something else. People who prefer to have open, straightforward dealings with others will often restrict their contact with you to a minimum. So the pattern looks like this:

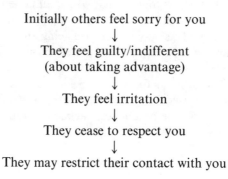

Initially others feel sorry for you
↓
They feel guilty/indifferent
(about taking advantage)
↓
They feel irritation
↓
They cease to respect you
↓
They may restrict their contact with you

It is a strange paradox that the person who sets out to please, to be liked, and who behaves nonassertively to achieve this, often ends up being less respected than the aggressive person—who may not care whether they are liked or not!

EFFECTS ON ORGANIZATIONS

The effects already outlined are undesirable for the individuals involved. We believe there are also undesirable effects on organizations. So when an organization has many managers and specialists behaving nonassertively it will find that many of those effects on the outcomes of situations (described earlier) will occur frequently. For example:

- Conflicts will not be handled to the satisfaction of both parties. For instance, managers may not represent the best interests of the company to customers, or to suppliers
- Difficult decisions may well be avoided altogether, or delayed for too long, or else they will not be implemented successfully

- Problems will not be tackled early on but will increase almost beyond control
- Fewer initiatives will be taken, so that out-dated methods will be retained and opportunities will be lost

In addition, the organization might well end up with groups of staff who do not respect other groups of staff for their nonassertion: 'Why can't senior managers take a stand for once?' The danger is that sooner or later senior managers will over-react with aggression, in order to re-establish some authority. Or they will choose the wrong issue on which to take a stand.

You might be saying to yourself, 'If nonassertion has many undesirable effects, how come I (or other people) sometimes behave nonassertively?'

How you come to be nonassertive

We have already said that one reason for becoming nonassertive is that you may experience immediate pleasant effects which reinforce your nonassertion. Also, other people may reinforce your nonassertion. In addition, some organizations, either unwittingly or otherwise, encourage nonassertion, for instance through a climate that discourages questioning or trying new approaches. Let us now examine some of the other reasons for nonassertion.

FEAR OF UNPLEASANT CONSEQUENCES FROM ASSERTION
You may be afraid of what might happen if you were to behave assertively in a situation. For instance, when wanting to say 'No' to a colleague's request you may be afraid that she will cease to like you or she will become angry or upset. At other times you may be anxious about having an argument, losing your job, making changes to the status quo, facing uncertainty, and so on. We have found that fear of negative consequences is a common reason for people behaving nonassertively. Such anxiety will diminish only after you have behaved assertively and have not experienced these consequences.

PERCEIVING SITUATIONS OR OTHER PEOPLE AS THREATENING
Supposing you are unsure of your ability, say, to do your job; then you would want to avoid bringing attention to yourself and would thus try to adopt a 'low profile'. So any situation, such as a meeting, that looks to be bringing you into 'public' focus, you would see as threatening. Any person making reference to your work—maybe your manager checking whether you will meet your deadlines—you would see as threatening. This could result in your behaving nonassertively by:

- Saying little in meetings
- Failing to mention problems you are having in meeting your deadlines

FAILING TO ACCEPT YOUR ASSERTIVE RIGHTS

If you do not realize or fully accept that you have certain rights, then you will not stand up for these rights. So, for example, if you do not accept that you have the right to propose to senior management some changes to a particular work procedure, then you may complain to colleagues about it, but you will not raise it with senior managers—you will be nonassertive.

FAILING TO THINK RATIONALLY ABOUT YOURSELF

This often comes about when you frequently compare yourself unfavourably to other people. An example of this would be saying things like: 'I'll never be as good as Pete at getting my ideas across.' This may or may not be true, but it will probably lead you to put your ideas forward tentatively and to withdraw them at the first sign of resistance. So then your idea stands a good chance of being rejected—which confirms your first statement about yourself! Thinking of this sort maintains your nonassertion.

CONFUSING ASSERTION AND AGGRESSION

If you are brought up in an environment where nonassertion is common, you would be likely to see any firm statement of assertion from others as aggression. Because you do not want to be seen as 'aggressive', you then bend over backwards to make sure this does not happen. You do this by being unduly deferential and apologetic. This may happen if you work for an organization that encourages certain groups of its staff to be nonassertive. The organization may do this because it does not realize that another alternative to being nonassertive is to be assertive rather than aggressive.

FAILING TO DEVELOP ASSERTIVE SKILLS

If you have been encouraged from early days to behave nonassertively, then these are the behaviours that you become skilled at using. As you only use assertive behaviours in 'safe' situations, you do not become skilled at such things as stating your own point of view when it is different from other people's. Alternatively, you may have had unpleasant experiences of assertion, and this has convinced you it is dangerous, or impractical, for everyone to state his needs, wants or opinions.

The result is that your behaviour pattern will contain a lot of nonassertion. Maybe there will be occasional bursts of aggression, when the tension resulting from this nonassertion becomes too much.

EQUATING NONASSERTION WITH POLITENESS

Like most of us, you have probably been brought up to be polite and considerate to others. The mistake that many people make is to believe that in order to be polite you need to be nonassertive. So, for instance, you would keep quiet rather than disagree with someone else's opinion, or shrug off

8

rather than accept a genuine piece of praise from a colleague; whereas it is in fact quite possible to disagree and/or accept praise in an assertive way that will not be seen as impolite or inconsiderate. It is both polite and assertive to thank people, or to apologize say, if you bump into them—it is nonassertive to apologize profusely for your own opinion or for needing someone to do some work for you.

CONFUSING NONASSERTION WITH HELPFULNESS
You may believe that when you are nonassertive you are actually being helpful to the other person. In fact, the reverse may well be true. Look at this example from social life. A friend asks you and some others whether you would prefer tea or coffee. Each of you in reply says 'I don't mind', and so at the end of the exercise the friend is no further forward in deciding which to make! In a work context a member of staff may say he does not mind when he takes his holidays, believing that he is being helpful by giving wide options, but his response does not give you specific information to plan the future workload. Not only this, but all too often people actually *do* have preferences—they do not state them because they are trying to be helpful. Later on these preferences may come to the surface when a decision is made that does not fit in with them.

Of course, there will be times when you genuinely do not have a preference and you can make this clear by behaving assertively and saying something like 'I am happy with any of those options'. This is quite different from having preferences or doubts which you keep quiet about at the time in order to be 'helpful'.

We will now explore the other side of the picture—aggression—examining the effects of this behaviour and how it comes about.

The effects of aggression

With aggression, as we have mentioned, you are aiming to win, if necessary at the expense of others. But as you do so, what effects does aggression have—on the outcome of the particular situation, on yourself, on other people, and on the organization?

EFFECTS OF AGGRESSION ON THE OUTCOME OF THE SITUATION
We will return to an example we have used several times in the chapter. Your manager asks you to complete some additional work; you are the best person to do the work; but you have no spare time available. An aggressive response to this was 'What? I'm up to my eyes in work already. There's no way I can do that!' As a result of this particular aggression the outcome is likely to go one of two ways. Your manager may end up not having the work done by you at all—an unsatisfactory outcome because it does not appear to meet his

needs. Alternatively, he may become aggressive in return, saying something like 'Well, that's your problem', and pushing the work on to you regardless. This is not a satisfactory outcome either, because it does not meet your needs. So either way the outcome is not satisfactory in meeting both sets of needs. In addition, the outcome, whichever way it goes, will be of low quality because the work will probably suffer.

In many situations your aggression will produce outcomes that do not meet both sets of needs, and that are poor quality in themselves—a hasty decision, important issues getting lost, potentially useful ideas being stifled, or solutions that create further problems.

EFFECTS OF AGGRESSION ON YOU

Short-term effects
Immediately after behaving aggressively you may feel a reduction in tension owing to the release of pent-up emotions. For instance, have you ever been aware of anger building up inside yourself and, after expressing this anger, have you said to yourself 'I feel better for having said that?'

Where the aggression is successful in achieving what you want (getting your needs met), then you may feel a sense of power over others. Both this and the reduction in tension are pleasant experiences and serve to reinforce your aggressive behaviours.

Other people praising you may also serve to reinforce your aggression. For example, they may say such things as: 'You certainly told him where to get off', or 'I liked the way you put him in his place'.

There is the same dilemma as for nonassertion. The short-term consequences are pleasant and rewarding for you, while the long-term ones may well be undesirable for yourself, for other people, and for your organization. Let us look at what these are.

Longer-term effects
One of the effects is that after a while you may experience feelings of guilt or shame. This is particularly likely to occur if you more commonly behave nonassertively, only breaking into aggression from time to time. These feelings of guilt may lead you to try to make amends to the people on the receiving end of your aggression by being unduly apologetic or by being over-helpful for a while.

Instead of feeling guilt or embarrassment about your aggression you may start blaming it on other people. When you do this you will likely be in a constant state of alert, always guarding against attack from others. For instance, you may have found yourself using considerable energy, either before or during a meeting, to protect your position or your department, saying things like 'They'll be wanting to make changes. I mustn't let them'. Doubtless by the end of the day you'll be drained of energy.

10

Over a period of time you may well start generalizing that people are out to get you or to get one up on you (not just the people directly affected by your aggression). This can lead you to experience deepseated hate or mistrust for large groups of people ('You've got to watch sales people, they're always trying to pull a fast one'). You may even feel a rage against the human race ('Everybody wants something for nothing these days'). These strong feelings can leave you feeling isolated. Alongside this, you may find it difficult to maintain friendships; you may weaken your job prospects in an organization that does not encourage aggression; or you may suffer high blood pressure. So the longer-term effect of aggression on you follows this sort of pattern:

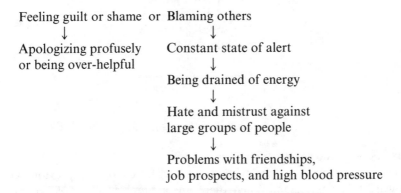

Feeling guilt or shame or Blaming others
    ↓   ↓
Apologizing profusely   Constant state of alert
or being over-helpful   ↓
                     Being drained of energy
                     ↓
                     Hate and mistrust against
                     large groups of people
                     ↓
                     Problems with friendships,
                     job prospects, and high blood pressure

As with nonassertion, the longer-term effects on you are undesirable but, because the short-term effects may be pleasant and rewarding, the aggression continues.

EFFECTS OF AGGRESSION ON OTHERS
For a while some people may feel admiration for you. Even people on the receiving end of your aggression may say things like 'He quite rightly tore me off a strip'. The admiration is not only for your aggression but also for themselves surviving in this 'tough' environment. However, more usually the person on the end of your aggression feels, angry, hurt, or humiliated, feelings that lead them to want to retaliate either openly or 'underground'. When people retaliate openly—with aggressive retorts, threats, deliberate mistakes, strikes, or go-slows—then it can be clearly seen that aggression breeds aggression.

When people go underground they may retaliate by withholding information, by making sarcastic comments behind your back, or by saying one thing to your face but doing something different. An example of the latter is people quietly making it difficult for your ideas to work out in practice. The people using underground retaliation are ones for whom open retaliation may be too risky, for example staff junior to you.

11

Without necessarily realizing it, some of your staff may take fewer initiatives as a result of your aggression and may form the habit of referring decisions to you. This is because they are not prepared to risk your aggression if their initiative did not meet your approval or their decision was wrong.

In the longer term, other people will either become resigned to you (probably behaving nonassertively in the face of your aggression), or they will leave and get a job elsewhere.

Thus the effect of aggression on others is along the following pattern:

Others may   or   They may feel anger,
admire you   hurt or humiliation
↓
They retaliate openly or
go underground
↓
They take fewer initiatives
or
↙   ↘
They become resigned   They leave

EFFECTS OF AGGRESSION ON ORGANIZATIONS

The organization as a whole is adversely affected by the previous consequences of aggression. When there are a number of people behaving aggressively the effects are multiplied. In particular, the organization may lose some talented and questioning people who, after a few early clashes, decide they are not prepared to work in such an aggressive environment. The staff who stay are likely to take fewer initiatives and risks, and to keep quiet about their ideas or doubts.

A problem we have encountered in several organizations concerns one-way aggressiveness from senior managers to junior managers. Here the dilemma is for junior staff newly promoted to their first management job. They are expected to continue being nonassertive (even deferential) to their aggressive seniors, but also to become aggressive with their own staff. Unfortunately, these junior managers find it difficult to suddenly swing to aggression because all their working life they have behaved nonassertively.

An organization may also suffer when some of its managers behave aggressively towards each other. This will result in more energy being put into beating each other (often referred to as 'playing politics') and less into cracking the problems they face. This may show itself in managers taking decisions (such as extensive 'empire-building') that are in their own or their department's interests but not in the interests of the organization.

Such 'in-fighting' may leave less time for attending to customer's needs, both immediate and longer-term. It is not uncommon for organizations to find that, over time, their base in the market place becomes eroded.

So, there are many undesirable effects of aggression, not only for the people involved but also for the organization. Let us now look at what may be leading you or others to behave aggressively.

How you come to be aggressive

As we have already said, there are a number of short-term 'rewards' that, in spite of any longer-term undesirable effects, will reinforce your aggression. There may even be longer-term rewards for aggression, such as organizations either deliberately or unwittingly encouraging aggression by promoting managers who behave aggressively. This is likely to happen where aggressive managers move on after a couple of years before the longer-term effects of their aggression become apparent. In addition, there are reasons for aggression. We describe some of these in the following sections.

PERCEIVING SITUATIONS OR OTHER PEOPLE AS THREATENING

We said earlier that, if you feel threatened by a situation or by someone, then you may behave nonassertively. However, an alternative way to protect yourself in the face of threat is to 'hit out', hence the saying 'attack is the best form of defence'.

The threat itself comes in several forms. It may be an *actual* attack from someone, for instance in a meeting a colleague saying: 'What on earth makes you think that'll work?—That's a crazy idea.' It may be a *perceived* attack. A good example of this is a person giving a presentation and being unsure of his material. He sees a 'genuine' question, to which he does not know the answer, as an attempt to show him up. He may well hit back with a sarcastic comment to hide his ignorance: 'If you'd been listening earlier, you wouldn't need to ask that.' The threat may come from an *anticipated* attack from someone. Let us suppose you have failed to meet a particular deadline. You expect to be taken to task by your manager in the review meeting next day. So you brace yourself for this and go into the meeting ready to go into the attack.

BELIEVING THAT AGGRESSION IS THE BEST APPROACH

If you believe that the only way to get results is to be aggressive, and you want to get results, then you will behave aggressively. Such a belief stems from seeing the world as a hostile place, in which the only way to survive is to 'get them before they get you'. We have come across a number of managers who hold these beliefs as well as organizations that encourage managers in these beliefs.

13

It is a self-fulfilling prophecy that, if you behave aggressively towards staff and colleagues, then they are likely to behave aggressively in return. The spiral of aggression is set up, so that the world of work does indeed become a hostile place.

In addition, you may see nonassertion as the only alternative to aggression. This leads you to make statements like 'Either you run your staff, or they run you'. You can see that you may survive in such a hostile environment by behaving nonassertively, but you reckon you will probably not progress. So you hold on to your aggressive behaviour. As we see it, the flaw in this thinking is that it denies or ignores the option of behaving assertively.

EARLIER NONASSERTION

When you have been nonassertive about something for a period of time, frustration, hurt, or anger can build up within you until you are not prepared to stand it any longer. You express your anger or defiance aggressively, often blaming others for the results of your nonassertion: 'I'm sick and tired of you asking me to do the boring jobs.' Other people may be perplexed by the sudden outburst because they have not necessarily behaved any differently towards you. They are probably not aware that this was 'the last straw'.

Another common way in which nonassertion and aggression are linked is when you behave nonassertively towards people with greater authority, often stifling the frustration or anger you feel as a result. You may then express these feelings by behaving aggressively towards people over whom you have some authority. For instance, if you have taken on more work from your manager than your department can handle you may then behave aggressively to your staff when they complain of the impossible workload.

OVER-REACTING BECAUSE OF A PREVIOUS EXPERIENCE

Sometimes you respond to a present situation with emotions that are left over from a past incident. So, strong feelings of resentment towards a colleague resulting from an incident yesterday can lead you to make aggressive comments about him to another colleague today, e.g. 'Don't talk to me about Fred . . .'.

FAILING TO THINK RATIONALLY ABOUT YOURSELF

This can happen when you frequently compare yourself with others. Sometimes the comparisons you make will be exaggerated unfavourably against you and will lead you to feel jealousy or resentment against others. This will result in your behaving aggressively towards them, maybe making sarcastic remarks against a particularly competent member of staff. At other times the comparisons you make will be exaggerated in your favour and will lead you to boast to other people: 'I really took the whole show there.' You might even criticize other people with negative comparison; for instance, 'How come you didn't get the same response I got from the customer?'

FAILING TO DEVELOP ASSERTIVE SKILLS

If the environment in which you work or have been brought up has encouraged you to use lots of aggressive behaviours, then these are the behaviours you become skilled at. (You may become expert at making people look small, or the master of the sarcastic aside.) You may not have developed, or may have lost through lack of practice, the skills to be successfully assertive.

Having read this section on aggression, some of you may be saying to yourself such things as: 'But surely aggression works, doesn't it?' or 'How do you explain that a lot of top managers are aggressive?' We would like to look at each of these questions in turn.

But surely aggression works ... doesn't it?

Yes, aggression *can* work in some situations. By working we mean that you achieve your objectives, you get what you want out of a situation or you get things moving. However, this is usually at a price. This price includes the negative effects, often in terms of the relationship, that we have outlined in the previous section. Before deciding that you are prepared to pay this price, it is useful to examine whether aggression works as often as you may believe.

We believe that aggression is most likely to work in situations where you have authority or power over the other person. The people working directly for you are the ones most likely to fall into this category. It is less likely to work with colleagues and very unlikely to work with people senior to you. Hence, if you are a specialist with no one directly responsible to you, you will not find aggression a very useful behaviour. Even if you are a manager with people working for you, your interactions with them may well be only a minority of your total interactions. In addition, these interactions may not be the crucial ones for your department's effectiveness. The level of cooperation that you receive from a colleague's department may be the crucial factor, and aggression may be a hindrance rather than a help when you are discussing this with your colleague.

It is also worth adding that aggressive behaviour with staff may be a declining asset. Fewer people are now prepared to put up with aggression compared with say 20 years ago. This trend is likely to continue and will be reinforced in certain jobs or industries by the demographic changes and skill shortages that are going to occur in the 1990s.

So we see aggression as being a limited option, as well as a high-risk one. Well worth trying the assertive option first, as we believe it can achieve better

15

or equally good results in the short run and better results in the long run—all without the undesirable side effects that come with aggression.

How do you explain that a lot of top managers are aggressive?

On the surface it may look that way. You see some senior people behaving aggressively, therefore it's easy to deduce that they have got there because of their aggression.

However, there are a number of flaws in this argument. It assumes that these people have been promoted *solely* because of their aggressive behaviour. It ignores the possibility that they may have been promoted *in spite of their aggressive behaviour*, not because of it. This alternative view is supported by conversations we have had, in which it has been made clear to us (and to the person in question) that what is holding an individual back is their tendency to blow up or create resentment. A second flaw concerns the way people notice, recall, and interpet instances of aggression. So in a meeting run by a senior manager, you witness him being very aggressive with another manager, really hauling him over the coals for missing a deadline. This 30-second exchange makes an impression on you, you tell your colleagues about it when you see them later on. The picture that emerges for them and for you is of an aggressive senior manager. This picture is based upon 30 seconds of a person's behaviour during say a two-hour meeting. So aggression could be the exception not the rule for this person. However, the organization grapevine may paint him as aggressive.

The problem can be compounded by the *interpretation* that people put upon these instances of aggression, when they are relayed or recalled. They tend to assume a connection between aggression and success. This is because the focus is upon the aggressive behaviour and not upon the outcome. It is quite likely that the aggressive behaviour was not very effective in sorting out the problem or contributing to a decision. However, this is seldom discussed. The worry therefore, is that you or other people may be modelling yourself on senior managers when they are not being effective. They may be at their least effective when they are being aggressive.

None of this is to deny that some senior managers behave aggressively some of the time, and in certain organizations certain individual senior managers may behave aggressively for much of the time. However, as we have pointed out it is easy to exaggerate both the amount of aggression and also its effectiveness. In addition, people make assumptions about aggressive behaviour being the reason for someone getting to a senior position. Once we get aggression into perspective, then we can see that some people reach the top without using much aggression. In other words for some people there is another way and it is the alternative route of assertion that we would now like to turn to.

Why be more assertive?

The short answer to this is that we believe behaving more assertively will result in your being more effective in your job. This is because assertion tends to breed assertion, so people are more likely to keep working *with* you rather than *against* you. In turn, this makes it easier to get satisfactory outcomes to many of the situations you have to handle. Let us illustrate this by returning to the examples we have used at various stages in the chapter. Your manager has asked you to complete some additional work. You are the best person to do the work but you have no spare time. As assertive response would be: 'I appreciate that you would like this work completed by the end of the month. However, I don't see I can fit it in with our workload as it is at present.' As a result of this particular assertion we predict that the outcome of the situation will be that you agree to take on the manager's additional work and he agrees to make changes to the workload. Because you are the best person to do the work, we would regard this as a high-quality outcome.

In many other situations it will also be important to get outcomes that are of a high quality—solutions that are workable, procedures that can readily be implemented, agreements that are clearly understood. Below we list a number of situations from which you will probably want to get 'good' outcomes or results.

- Coping with an angry customer, without making promises you cannot keep
- Asking your manager for a regrading to reflect the extra responsibilities you have taken on
- Having to make important arrangements over the telephone with a colleague who goes on at great length and is difficult to pin down
- Conveying 'bad news' to senior management
- Saying 'No' to unreasonable requests from colleagues, staff, or senior managers
- Disagreeing with the views of others in a meeting, without causing resentment
- Carrying out an appraisal with a member of staff who believes she is ready for promotion when you do not think she is
- Chasing people up who have promised to do something for you as a favour and then have not done it
- Reaching agreement with a colleague who is behaving aggressively so that you feel you stood your ground without becoming aggressive in return

We believe that behaving assertively in these and other situations will help you achieve effective outcomes in these situations. These will contribute to your increasing your overall effectiveness. In addition, assertion has other benefits, some of which we explain in the following sections.

17

AN INCREASED CHANCE OF NEEDS BEING MET

If you are behaving more assertively, you are stating more clearly what your needs, wants, ideas, and opinions are. This by itself increases the chances that your needs will be met and your opinions taken into account.

At the same time, because assertion is about not ignoring or dismissing the needs and wants of others, you will encourage others to make their needs known. If there is no conflict between their needs and yours, then you have increased the chances that these too will be met. Where the needs that emerge are in conflict, then we believe assertive behaviour helps individuals to find solutions that are acceptable to both persons. More detail on this is given in Chapter 11.

GREATER CONFIDENCE IN YOURSELF

We do recognize, however, that in some instances your needs may not be fully met. Indeed, in some cases they may not be met at all. The important point here is that, even if this should happen, because you have made your needs or views known, you are more likely to feel 'OK' about yourself and the situation. Afterwards you will say to yourself such things as: 'I stood up to Helen, and said what I had to say in a reasonable manner.'

Feeling OK about a situation enables you to put it behind you as opposed to replaying it over and over in your mind ('I wish I'd spoken up. What I should have said was ...'). This takes up valuable time and energy and leaves you with less confidence to face up the the next tricky situation.

Handling difficult situations to your satisfaction will lead you to say to yourself, 'I can get John to listen to my ideas' or 'I can talk to my staff about their performance when it is not up to par, without creating ill feeling between us'.

This will lead you to have a *healthy* regard for yourself, your skills and abilities. (This is not to be confused with boastfulness, e.g. 'I'm the best at ...', which is aggression.) There is a snowball effect here in that behaving assertively leads to greater self-confidence, which in turn leads to more assertive behaviour.

GREATER CONFIDENCE IN OTHERS

Increased confidence about yourself helps you to recognize and accept the strengths of those who work with or for you, rather than being threatened by them. So you use the strength that a particular member of your staff has for giving presentations. At the same time you will be more open about their limitations. Thus, in delegating to them, for example, you would not do it in a reckless way, which ignores their lack of experience in this new area, but in a planned, realistic way that recognizes any limitation on their performance. Handling it in this way enables you to feel confident that the task will be carried out satisfactorily.

INCREASED RESPONSIBILITY FOR YOUR OWN BEHAVIOUR

Being more assertive involves you taking more responsibility for your own behaviour. This leads in turn to your being more in control of your behaviour. So you move away from blaming other people for your behaviour; you no longer say things like: 'I couldn't help myself. After he brought up the issue of overtime again, I just blew my top.'

Increasing your assertion leads you to recognize that you have more control over how you respond to such incidents than you previously thought. At the same time, you realize that if you 'cannot stop yourself' from responding with aggression in such situations, then you are handing control of your behaviour over to the other person. He begins to see that he only has to mention overtime to get you to 'blow your top'.

Initially you may doubt that you can learn to control your own behaviour. 'It's only natural to respond aggressively in such situations', you say. Our experience is that people can increase their control by the techniques described in this book.

TAKING MORE INITIATIVES

If you are to influence the environment in which you work, it is not enough just to react to situations as they occur. It is necessary and important to take initiatives to make or stop certain situations occurring. These initiatives may be small—for example, putting forward an idea in a meeting—or large—such as changing the flow of work through your department.

If you behave assertively you are more likely to take such initiatives, because you are not afraid of failure or of making a mistake. You do not want to fail and will work hard to get it right. However, you recognize that from time to time an initiative will fail, but that you can acknowledge and cope with this failure. You do not let the risk of failure stop you taking the initiative as people behaving nonassertively do. Neither do you try and blame others or pretend that it was not a failure, as the person behaving aggressively does.

A SAVING IN ENERGY

Because you are no longer preoccupied with not upsetting others, and no longer so concerned about losing out, you will be able to save yourself a lot of nervous energy. For instance, no longer will you be worrying about how to tell a member of staff that he has not got the promotion he was expecting, or planning how to get back at somebody who tried to show you up in a meeting yesterday.

You will also experience a reduction in stress and tension associated with getting results. For example, you will find taking decisions less stressful because you will be less concerned with what other people think and with the fear of making a mistake.

19

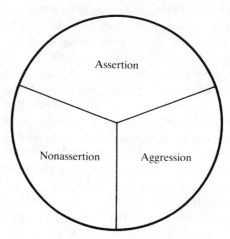

Figure 1.1   Behaviour options

Using less energy in these negative ways leaves you more energy to use productively in other areas of your job.

Some concluding considerations

NO ONE IS LIKELY TO BEHAVE AGGRESSIVELY OR NONASSERTIVELY ALL THE TIME

Each person's behaviour is likely to be a mixture of the three options available. The size of the segments in the pie chart below will be different for different people. We may, however, be able to make certain generalizations. For example, in Figure 1.1 a pie chart representing managers' interactions with their senior managers will have a larger nonassertion segment than one representing their interactions with their staff. It follows that, strictly speaking, it is incorrect to talk of an aggressive or nonassertive person. We really prefer to say that a person was behaving aggressively or nonassertively in a particular situation.

YOUR ASSERTION MAY BREAK DOWN IN DIFFICULT SITUATIONS

It is likely that for you and many people holding down a job in an organization the assertion segment of the pie chart in Figure 1.1 will certainly be substantial. You will be using assertive behaviours much of the time. It is during what you perceive to be difficult situations that the aggressive or nonassertive behaviours come to the fore. So being more assertive is about *spreading* your assertive behaviour into these difficult situations.

NONASSERTION AND AGGRESSION OFTEN COME FROM THE SAME SOURCE

Much evidence and our own experience suggests that both nonassertion and low self-esteem aggression spring from low esteem. Your self-esteem is the evaluation that you make and hold about yourself. It is *your* judgement of *your* worth as a person. It is based upon the extent to which you believe yourself to be a competent, significant, likeable, and successful person.

If your self-esteem is low, then you will feel an uncomfortable degree of anxiety in certain situations. You will feel threatened by that situation and the people in it. When you feel threatened you either hit out (agg) or you 'turn into yourself' for protection (na).

So the sequence is:

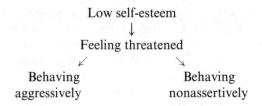

It is important to stress this point that low self-esteem can lead to aggression as well as to nonassertion. You may find this surprising particularly because many people behaving aggressively have an outward appearance of over-confidence and self-assuredness. This outward aggression is often a mask for the insecurity that comes from unhealthy self-regard or low esteem. You may have noticed how this mask can drop when someone stands up to this person. The aggression crumbles and is replaced by nonassertion, say in the form of excessive apologizing.

BEING ASSERTIVE IS DEALING WITH ISSUES WHEN THEY ARE SMALL

We believe that if you can deal with issues and problems when they are small, then you will have fewer of the 'big blow ups' that are so draining, and difficult to resolve. You will also be more successful in resolving these issues. Once problems have been around a while and grown in size and importance they are more difficult to resolve—not only because they are more complex, but also because the people involved have had more time to take up entrenched positions. So, for instance, dealing with a sarcastic comment as and when it is made may well save a more aggressive exchange later on.

In this chapter we have introduced the concepts of assertiveness. Many of the themes, like rights and negative feelings, will be developed in later chapters, as will practical applications of the concepts.

2. Recognizing assertive, nonassertive and aggressive behaviour

In the previous chapter we included definitions of ass, agg, and na. If you want to use more assertive behaviour (and at this point we will assume you do), then an essential step towards this is for you to be able to recognize when you and others are actually using ass, agg, or na. But the definitions we used were global statements about these three types of behaviour; they were only a start point in the process of recognizing the three types. So in this chapter we will make more specific distinctions between ass, agg, and na. For each of the three types we describe the *verbal* behaviour used and then give a recognition exercise for you to work through. Following this, we look at the *nonverbal* aspects of the three types.

Verbal aspects of behaviour

By this we mean *what* people say: the message they convey and the words they use. We are not here concerned with *how* people say it. So in the next three sections we describe the statements and questions people use for each of the three behaviour types and give examples of them.

VERBAL ASPECTS OF ASSERTION
Just to recap, assertive behaviour is standing up for your own rights, wants, needs, and beliefs without violating those of other people. So, people behaving assertively are likely to use the following:

- 'I' statements, like: 'I think ...'; 'My idea is ...'; 'I want ...'; 'I'd like to ...'; 'I prefer ...'; 'I feel ...'. These indicate that the person is speaking for themself rather than for some unidentified entity such as 'the department'. So: 'I'd like to change the procedure' rather than 'It would be a good idea to change the procedure'
- Statements that are brief and to the point: 'I'd like to get started this week'. From this, it is clear what you want. By contrast, long rambling statements confuse the other person, leaving him unclear about what you want
- Distinctions between fact and opinion: 'As I see it ...'; 'My opinion is...'; 'My experience is different in that ...'. This recognizes that things are not

always 'black and white', 'good or bad', but that they can be different for different people. So: 'The system works well for me' rather than 'The system is good'

- Suggestions (for how the other person could proceed) that *do not* contain heavily weighted 'advice': 'How about tackling it this way?'; 'Would it be practical to ...?'; 'Would you like to ...?'. These enable the other person to make up their own mind after evaluating the suggestions for themselves
- Constructive 'criticism', which states the facts of people's actions without attacking them as people: 'Colin, I've noticed your reports have not been coming in on time.' There is no excessive blaming here or jumping to conclusions
- Questions to find out the thoughts, opinions and wants of others: 'How does that fit in with your plans?'; 'What will this involve?'; 'What are your thoughts on ...'. More use is made of 'open-ended' questions (i.e. ones that require more than a yes/no answer) to get more information back. 'Leading' questions (that push the other person into making the 'approved' response) are avoided: 'You do delegate work, don't you?'
- Behaviours for getting round problems: 'Let's look for a way to overcome that', 'How can we get around that?' 'Shall we... ?'

These words and phrases differ from ones that people use when they are being nonassertive or aggressive.

VERBAL ASPECTS OF NONASSERTION
As we have said, nonassertive behaviour is failing to stand up for your rights, needs, and wants, or doing so in ways that make it easy for other people to violate them. So, people behaving nonassertively are likely to use the following:

- Rambling statements—sometimes long and complex, sometimes tailing off at the end: 'I thought you might like to ... er ... well ...'. These either take a circuitous route to mentioning the subject under discussion, or fail to mention it at all (perhaps in the hope that the other person will do so)
- Fill-in words and hesitant phrases: 'Uh'; '... you know what I mean'; 'well ... like'; 'only'; 'just'; 'maybe'; 'er ... erm'. These often show that the speaker is camouflaging the message or gathering courage to deliver it
- Frequent justifications of themselves: 'I wouldn't normally mention this only ...'; 'I was just going past your door so I thought I'd see whether ...'. These justifications are often meant to weaken the impact of the speaker's behaviour and reduce the chances of other people perceiving it as 'bold'. They usually point to a confusion between assertiveness and aggressiveness
- Profuse apologies, and statements 'seeking permission': 'I'm terribly sorry, I really didn't meant to ...'; 'I'm very sorry to bother you'; 'I hope

23

you don't really mind but would it be all right if ...'; 'Excuse me please, but can we ...'. Many of these indicate confusion between politeness and nonassertion. It's polite to apologize after spilling beer over someone; it's na to do so *profusely* like a 'whipped dog', or to apologize in advance for some anticipated 'misdemeanour'. People constantly 'seeking permission' have handed over control for themselves to others

- Self-regulatory statments: 'I should'; 'I must'; 'I ought to get on with X'; 'I have to ...'. These indicate that the person has handed over control to an outside force whom he feels duty bound to obey. The force may be parents, spouse, colleague, manager, department, etc
- Few 'I' statements, and usually with qualifiers: 'It's only my opinion but ...'; 'I think it will work, but I might be wrong'. These qualifiers downplay the fact that the person is speaking for themselves, and also make it less likely that others will challenge their view
- Phrases that dismiss their own needs and wants: 'I could do with some extra time but it doesn't matter really'; '... but it's not important'; 'Yes, but don't worry, I'll manage'. These reduce risk of an outright refusal which would be embarrassing or hurtful. They invite the other person to ignore the needs and wants
- Phrases that put themselves down: 'I'm hopeless at this'; 'You know me, I seem to be useless at ...'; 'I can't seem to ...'. These often invite a denial and even a pat on the back from the other person. Sometimes the person using these phrases will wallow in self-despair instead of making changes that will overcome whatever deficiency exists

People using the above statements would be raising issues and responding to other people, albeit tentatively or self-deprecatingly. In addition to this, people frequently behave nonassertively by saying *nothing*. They will fail to raise issues that concern them; they will keep quiet about their doubts and disagreements.

The words and phrases used above contrast with ones that people use when they are being aggressive.

VERBAL ASPECTS OF AGGRESSION

Aggressive behaviour, as we have stated, is standing up for your own rights, needs, wants, and beliefs in ways that violate or ignore those of other people. So people behaving aggressively are likely to use the following:

- An excess of 'I' statements with heavy emphasis on the 'I' part: '*I* think it will work'; '*My* view is that ...'; '*I'd* like ...'. This emphasis infers that the speaker's view is more important, which deters other people from challenging it
- Boastfulness: '*My* projects are *always* on time.' Here the negative comparison of other people is *implied*, at other times it is stated: '*I* never have any problems with this, not like *you*'

- Opinions expressed as facts: 'That won't work'; 'Nobody wants to do that'; 'That procedure is useless'. These indicate that the person is speaking for everyone, basing their judgement on their own experience and ignoring other people's experience
- Threatening questions: 'Why on earth did you do *that*?'; 'Haven't you come up with a solution yet?' These unnerve the other person by 'putting him on the spot'. The questions turn an interaction into an inquisition
- Requests in the form of instructions or even threats: 'You'd *better* do that'; 'I *want* that information *straightaway*'; 'That report *has* to be finished by tomorrow, or else'. A threat may be spoken or implied, but in any case the instructions alone mean that the person is trying to control the other person
- Heavily weighted advice for how the other person could proceed: 'You should do it this way'; 'You must pull your socks up'; 'You ought'; 'You have to'. All these are quoting some hidden 'rule book' that controls the other person. They imply a moral judgement of 'bad', 'wrong', 'wicked' on whoever disobeys. Sometimes the advice is of the fatherly sort, with plenty of well-meant persuasion: 'If I were you ...'; 'Why don't you ...'. All of these suggestions, both fatherly and otherwise, reduce the chances of the other person evaluating the suggestions for themselves and making up their own mind
- Blame for past events, often with no constructive statements about change: 'It wouldn't have happened if you hadn't been so ...'; 'You made a mess of that'; 'Well, I blame the youth/workers/management of today'; 'Your attitude is all wrong'. These generalized comments do not highlight specific cause and effects of behaviour. It is difficult for the other person to do anything about a general disorder like a 'mess' or an 'attitude'; and the excessive blaming makes it unlikely that he would want to anyway
- Assumptions about people and events: 'I don't suppose you've done X'; 'Presumably you won't want much time for this'; 'Production missed the deadlines, as usual'. These assumptions stem from notions of 'I know you better than you do' or 'These people are always the same'
- Sarcasm and similar statements: 'You must be joking'; 'That's only *your* opinion'; 'That's rubbish'. These put the other person down by dismissing their opinions, suggestions or needs

In the last three sections we have described the verbal aspects of ass, na, and agg. You have probably been saying various things to yourself like: 'Hm, that sounds like me' or 'My manager/colleague says things like that'. This is fine from our point of view, because it means you are probably keen to go on now and spot examples of ass, na, and agg behaviours as they actually occur. But before doing this, if you want to make sure you can distinguish the three types of behaviour, on paper at least, then work through the recognition exercise, Table 2.2. As a 'memory jogger' for doing this, the chart in Table 2.1

Table 2.1 Summary of verbal aspects of behaviour

	Nonassertive	Assertive	Aggressive
Verbal content	• Long, rambling statements • Fill-in words: 'maybe' • Frequent justifications • Apologies and 'permission seekers' • 'I should', 'I ought' • Few 'I' statements (often qualified) • Phrases that dismiss own needs: 'not important really' • Self put-downs 'I'm hopeless'	• Statements that are brief, clear and to the point • 'I' statements: 'I'd like' • Distinctions between fact and opinion • Suggestions not weighted with 'advice' • No 'shoulds' nor 'oughts' • Constructive 'criticism' without blame or assumptions • Questions to find out the thoughts, opinions, wants of others • Ways for getting round problems	• Excess of 'I' statements • Boastfulness: 'My' • Opinions expressed as facts • Threatening questions • Requests as instructions or threats • Heavily weighted advice in the form of 'should' and 'ought' • Blame put on others • Assumptions • Sarcasm and other put-downs

Background to example

A colleague rings up when you are working on a report that you particularly want to finish. She says she wants to talk about next week's safety meeting. You prefer to discuss the matter later in the day.

	Nonassertive	Assertive	Aggressive
Your response	'Oh, I hope you don't mind but I'm a bit busy at the moment. Would it possibly be all right if I rang you back later this afternoon?' Or you discuss it there and then without making your preference known.	'Fine. I'm happy to talk about the safety meeting, but right now I'd like to finish this report. How about my ringing you back later this afternoon?'	'You can't expect me to think about a safety meeting. I'm in the middle of a report. You'll have to ring me back later.'

restates the verbal content of the three types of behaviour in a convenient form. At the end it gives an example of the same issue being raised in the three different ways: ass, na, and agg.

Recognition exercise: assertive, nonassertive and aggressive behaviours

The exercise in Table 2.2 contains 20 examples, each with a description of a situation followed by a response. You are asked to state whether each response is assertive (ass) nonassertive (na), or aggressive (agg).

Table 2.2   Recognition exercise

Answer	Situation	Response	Your answer
	1. The date is being set for the next meeting of the committee of which you are a member. You are keen to attend but the proposed date accepted by everyone else, means you cannot attend. When the chairperson says 'Is that OK for everyone, then?' You say:	'Well, all right, as it seems to be convenient to everyone else.'	
na	2. A colleague asks you for a lift home. It's inconvenient to you, as you are late already and the drive will take you out of your way. You say:	'I'm about 20 minutes late so I won't be able to take you home. If it helps I can drop you off at the nearest bus stop.'	
ass	3. You're having trouble getting started on a report. You can't see a logical starting point. You say to a colleague:	'I'm useless at writing reports. I can't really see how to even start it!'	
na	4. Your manager asks what went wrong when you were installing a new machine for a customer. You say:	'You wasted a lot of my time! You never even *told* me he didn't have the area ready.'	
agg	5. A member of staff interrupts you when you are making an important call to a supplier. You say:	'I'd like to finish this phone call, then I'll be happy to answer your question.'	
ass	6. Your secretary is arranging your diary for the day. She asks you 'What time will you be back in the office?' You say:	'Haven't a clue.'	
agg	7. A colleague hears you dealing with an awkward customer. Afterwards they praise the way you handled it. You say:	'Well, I only really came in at the end.'	
na	8. You sat in on a presentation given by one of your staff. You felt it was highly successful. You say:	'I think that was a really good presentation. I particularly liked the way you made the material come alive.'	

Table 2.2 (*Continued*)

Answer	Situation	Response	Your answer
ass	9. One of your staff is going to visit a client who is well known as a 'slippery character'. You know your subordinate is hesitant in his dealings with people. You say to him:	'You've *got* to stand up to him, Pete. Tell him what's acceptable to us. You *mustn't* let him get away with airy-fairy nonsense, like *last* time.'	
agg	10. A colleague has just produced a good work plan for their department. You'd like their help with one for your department. You say:	'That work plan, you produced is a good approach. Will you be able to spend half an hour working on one with me for my department?'	
ass	11. A member of staff tells you she is wanting to take responsibility for some of the enquiries. You say:	'What on earth for? You know jolly well you're struggling to keep up with the filing – without doing extra work.'	
agg	12. A salesman has been pushing hard for you to buy a piece of equipment. You are not too sure; besides, you had thought of looking at several makes before deciding. You say:	'Well, I suppose it's more or less what I'm looking for. I was going to look at other makes, but perhaps this will be OK.'	
na	13. A colleague in another department has volunteered your services without consulting you, to help a junior manager draw up their financial return! You say:	'Look, why didn't you ask me first, instead of dropping me in it?'	
agg	14. Your manager wants Pete, (one of your staff), to carry out a survey for her over the next two weeks. You really prefer Steve, another member of staff to do the survey. You say:	'Well, I don't know. Pete has just started a job for the Packer firm, but perhaps he could be taken off that. Steven won't be so good at the Packer job but I suppose I could always help him out.'	
na	15. A colleague agreed to come to a special meeting and then failed to turn up. You ring him and say:	'Dave, I understood you were coming to the meeting. I would have liked you to be there. What was the problem?'	

Table 2.2 (*Continued*)

Answer	Situation	Response	Your answer
ass	16. One of your staff (you don't know which one) forgot to list details of a customer's receipt. You are aware of this and say to your staff:	'Look here, somebody's forgotten to note the details of this receipt. I don't care who it is, I want it put right straight away.'	
agg	17. Your manager has sent a memo saying that no more business visits must be made without his prior agreement. You are unhappy with this and you say to him:	'Colin, I'm concerned about the new arrangement, 'cos I think it will create a number of problems for me. I'd like to discuss it with you.'	
ass	18. A member of staff has asked to take a day's holiday at a time when the department is working frantically to finish the monthly returns. You say:	'I hope you won't think I'm being mean, but Mr Cross will not like you to take time off tomorrow. I'm very sorry.'	
na	19. Your manager asks you to attend a meeting. The last time you went it wasn't relevant to your department so you don't want to go. You say:	'I'm really busy this week with schedules, I don't think I'll have time to go.'	
na	20. A colleague wants your advice on a non urgent issue. You're happy to help, but not at the moment as you want to finish a report before you go home. You say:	'I'm happy to help Jill, but it will need to be tomorrow as I want to finish this off before I go.'	
ass			

There is space for you to write your answer in the *right*-hand column. Our answer for each response is given in the *left*-hand column, on the *line below*. This enables you to check your own answer before moving on to the next example. This way you reduce the risk of making the same mistake more than once throughout the exercise. It is usually best to reveal only one example at a time, covering up the answer until you are ready to check it.

If you don't see why a response has been answered the way it has, please note this and check it out with the explanations we give at the end of the exercise (Table 2.3) or look back through the chapter at the detailed descriptions and examples.

Table 2.3   Comments on answers in recognition exercise

Ex. no.	Ans.	Comment
3	na	Putting yourself down—helplessness
4	agg	Blaming, jumping to conclusions (the manager may not have had the information)
6	agg	Ignores her need to know; you may not have the answer, but this doesn't give you the right to dismiss the question
7	na	Selling yourself short (also, incidentally, has the effect of devaluing the person's praise)
9	agg	Giving heavily weighted advice
10	ass	Straight acknowledgement of the colleague's work. Not pleading or putting yourself down; nor instructing him to give time to you
11	agg	Dismissing member of staff's wants, questioning her judgement
16	agg	'Straightaway' has an implied threat of 'or else'. 'Look here' is aggressive
18	na	Not taking any responsibility for the decision
19	na	Not 'coming clean'; giving excuse rather than real reason

If, with some of the examples in Table 2.2, you are wondering why we gave the answers we did, the comments in Table 2.3 will explain our thinking.

If you have worked through the examples in Table 2.2, or as a result of your experiences to date, you might be saying 'But isn't it *how* you say things that determines whether they come across as assertive, nonassertive or aggressive?' The answer is both Yes and No.

Let us deal with the 'No' first of all. Supposing (as in example 3 in the table) you say things like: 'I'm useless at writing reports'; then we see this as putting yourself down. It may be true, for instance, that when writing reports your language is not fluent, your arguments disorganized, but this does not necessarily add up to your being 'useless'. This would be understating your abilities—in our terms, behaving na. Alternatively (as in example 11), you might say to a member of staff something along the lines of: 'What on earth for? You know jolly well ...'. Then we regard this as dismissing the other person, denying her right to have wants and views that are different from your own—in other words, behaving agg. With these examples, we convey a message that would be more or less unchanged no matter *how* we say them. It is the words themselves that make these and many other examples into na or agg.

But 'Yes' sometimes it *does* depend on *how* we say things as to whether they are ass, agg, or na. Try saying the following statement (example 5) to yourself several times, each time putting the emphasis on different words or pausing from time to time. For instance,

1. *'I'd* like to finish this *phone* call; *then* I'll be happy to answer your *question.'*

2. '*I'd like* to finish this *phone call*; then I'll be *happy* to answer your *question*.'

3. 'I'd ... like to ... finish this ... phone call, then I'll ... be happy to ... answer your ... question.'

Recognizing the limitations of written words, we have tried to portray no. 1 as agg, no. 2 as ass, and no. 3 as na. Whether you picked up these intended distinctions or not, you probably noticed considerable differences in the message that came across as you said the same statement to yourself in several ways. These different messages were conveyed not as a result of the words themselves (these were unchanged), but as a result of the differences in *how* you *said* the words—the emphasis, the tone of voice, the hesitancies. These are examples of what we will call *nonverbal* behaviour.

Nonverbal aspects of ass, agg and na

By this we mean all the observable aspects of behaviour that accompany speech, apart from the words themselves. We include both audible and visible aspects, and the ones we have found to be important are the following:

Voice	The tone: sarcastic or sincere; warm or cold; rich and expressive or dull and flat
	The volume: shouting; barely audible; or medium volume
Speech pattern	Slow, hesitant, fast, jerky, abrupt, or steady even pace
Facial expression	Brow: wrinkled or smooth
	Eyebrows: raised, lowered, or level
	Jaw: set firm or relaxed
Eye contact	Whether the speaker looks at other people or the surroundings and for how long
Body movement	Movement with individual parts of the body, e.g. head, hands
	Movement and position of the whole body

WHY NONVERBAL BEHAVIOURS ARE IMPORTANT TO ASSERTIVENESS
We have already mentioned that some statements can be said in different ways and that it is the nonverbal behaviours (tone of voice, emphasis, etc.) that determine whether these statements come across as ass, agg, or na. But more important than this, for people who want to increase their assertiveness, is the notion that *nonverbal behaviours can undermine potentially assertive words*. Let us illustrate what we mean by this.

Suppose a colleague says the following potentially assertive statement to

31

you: 'I'd like to hear your thoughts on X'. He then looks at you with an open expression on his face, relaxed, and waiting for you to talk. You would be clear from all this that he wanted to listen carefully to your ideas. But suppose that, after making the statement, he folded his arms tightly across his chest, turned his body slightly away from you, stared at you with his chin thrust out and with his jaw tightly set. Would you still be certain that he was going to listen to you without pre-judging your ideas? Probably not.

So nonverbal behaviour can detract from and even override the verbal behaviour. If you want to behave assertively, you need to have the nonverbal aspects *in line* with the verbal aspects. If they are in line they give emphasis to your verbal assertions and increase the likelihood that your behaviour will come across to others as assertive.

We describe the nonverbal aspects associated with ass, agg, and na in Table 2.4 and in the sections that follow. However, if you are not sure how aware you are of nonverbal behaviour generally, it is a good idea to look out for the ones we have described so far before going into further detail. The next time you are in a pub or at work try observing a couple of people holding a conversation you are not involved in. Or when you find yourself stuck with a boring television programme take your own natural break and notice the nonverbal behaviours of the participants (particularly fascinating if you turn the sound down).

A word of caution

A single example say of 'finger pointing' does not necessarily add up to aggressive behaviour. In order to decide whether a behaviour is ass, agg, or na we might need to look at the other nonverbal behaviours being used. The examples in Table 2.4 are meant only as guidelines; many of them may well not be a part of your nonverbal 'repertoire', or you may have ones that are different from these. What is important is that you select the nonverbal behaviours that you believe are most preventing you from increasing your assertiveness and work at bringing these into your conscious control. In our experience no one has ever increased their assertiveness by globally bringing their nonverbal behaviours into line. But people have, for instance, improved their assertiveness by firming up on their eye contact, modifying their hand movements or speaking more slowly.

ADDITIONAL NOTES

You may already have a sufficient picture of the different nonverbal behaviours, in which case we suggest you skip the following comments.

Speech pattern

'Emphasizes key words' (ass) means speaking certain words, slowly, firmly and expressively, but not thumping them hard. The sorts of words to

Table 2.4   Nonverbal aspects of na, ass and agg

	Nonassertive	Assertive	Aggressive
Voice	• Sometimes wobbly • Tone may be singsong or whining • Over-soft or over-warm • Often dull and in monotone • Quiet, often drops away at end	• Steady and firm • Tone is middle range, rich and warm • Sincere and clear • Not over-loud or quiet	• Very firm • Tone is sarcastic sometimes cold • Hard and sharp • Strident, maybe shouting, rises at end
Speech pattern	• Hesitant and filled with pauses • Sometimes jerks from fast to slow • Frequent throat-clearing	• Fluent, few awkward hesitances • Emphasizes key words • Steady, even pace	• Fluent, few awkward hesitances • Often abrupt, clipped • Emphasizes blaming words • Often fast
Facial expression	• 'Ghost' smiles when expressing anger, or being criticized • Eyebrows raised in anticipation (e.g. of rebuke) • Quick-changing features	• Smiles when pleased • Frowns when angry Otherwise 'open' • Features steady, not wobbling • Jaw relaxed	• Smile may become 'wry' • Scowls when angry • Eyebrows raised in amazement/ disbelief • Jaw set firm • Chin thrust forward
Eye contact	• Evasive • Looking down	• Firm but not a 'stare-down'	• Tries to stare down and dominate
Body movements	• Hand-wringing • Hunching shoulders • Stepping back • Covering mouth with hand • Nervous movements which detract (shrugs and shuffles) • Arms crossed low for protection	• Open hand movements (inviting to speak) • 'Measured pace' hand movements • Sits upright or relaxed (not slouching or cowering) • Stands with head held up	• Finger pointing • Fist thumping • Sits upright or leans forward • Stands upright head 'in air' • Strides around (impatiently) • Arms crossed high (unapproachable)

emphasize would mostly be nouns and verbs that we want people to visualize or remember; e.g. 'I *think* the programme meets our *needs* but I'd *like* to take a couple of *days* to study it in *detail*.'

33

Facial expression

'Ghost' smiles (na) are the smiles that fleet across a person's face when they are under attack, or when they are criticizing the other person.

A 'wry' smile (agg) is the sort that accompanies sarcasm, when the mouth turns up at the corners.

'Quick changing features' (na) are where the face changes quickly from smiling to frowning within the same sentence. It gives the impression that the person has no control over facial expression.

Eye contact

This is one of the ways you regulate conversation. Have you noticed on the telephone how difficult it is to know whether the other person has finished speaking? You both need eye contact to tell each other when to come in, what each other's reactions are, whether there is understanding. You also need to look away from time to time, to collect your thoughts or to visualize things.

Body movements

In a sense, these are the way the body summarizes its behaviour. So with na there is a curling up in *protection from* the 'world'; with assertion there is a *standing up to face* the 'world'; and with agg there is a leaning forward in a point of *attack against* the world.

Summary

In this chapter we have said:

- Certain words and phrases are likely to be seen as assertive, nonassertive, or aggressive
- Certain nonverbal behaviours are associated with assertion, nonassertion, and aggression
- Nonverbal behaviours need to be in line with verbal behaviours in order to give emphasis to the verbal assertiveness
- Increased assertiveness comes about by concentrating on one specific aspect of verbal or nonverbal behaviour at a time

3. Beliefs and rights

You may well be familiar with the word 'rights', for instance in the context of company appraisals, where individuals often have the 'right' to appeal against a particular performance rating. Rights also occur in industrial relations, with management claiming the 'right' to manage and trade unions claiming the 'right' to be consulted. You may feel uneasy with the word 'rights' because it is often associated, especially in the latter context, with confrontation and aggression. But this need not be so. The problem lies not with the *concept* of rights as such, so much as with the *way people stand up* for their rights. Indeed, the dictionary definition, and the one we use, defines a right as simply 'something to which you are entitled'. Rights are a central issue to assertiveness. This is because our definition of assertiveness talks of standing up for your rights, wants, needs, and feelings without denying the rights, wants, needs, and feelings of others.

So the aim of the first part of this chapter is to enable you to be clear about the rights involved in situations you encounter. In the second part we look at beliefs and the way they influence the rights you accept for yourself and give to others.

Why rights are important to assertiveness

Rights are important because they are one of the bases for deciding whether *other people* are behaving aggressively, nonassertively or assertively towards you. Quite simply, if you do not know what your rights are then you will find it difficult to judge whether other people are violating those rights. Let us suppose your manager comes to you insisting that you forego one of your four holiday weeks. You know you have the right to four holiday weeks, so you can judge that your manager, by being insistent, is violating your rights—he or she is behaving aggressively. When you are able to make this sort of judgement, you can go on and decide how to stand up for your rights.

A second reason why rights are important is that *not* being clear on them makes it more difficult for *you* to behave assertively. Have you ever found yourself:

- Hesitating about raising an issue?
- Having decided to raise an issue but being unsure about 'how far to push' it?
- Being unsure of your ground but blustering your way through none-theless?

A friend told us of the time he returned a faulty tyre to the garage supplying it. The supplier said that if he wanted a replacement tyre free of charge he would have to wait for one from the manufacturers. Alternatively, they could fit one but would have to charge for the tyre. At this point he was unsure where he stood, so he reluctantly agreed to have a tyre from the manufacturer, which meant waiting at least a week. What happened here was that our friend was not clear whether he had the right to a free replacement tyre from the supplier or only from the manufacturer. Because of this he ended up dropping the issue (with some feelings of regret), and behaving nonassertively. So being clear on your rights and the rights of other people in any situation enables you to decide: whether other people are violating your rights, whether you are violating their rights, whether to raise a particular issue and how far to go.

What are my rights?

Before answering this question it is useful to say a few words about where rights come from. The concept of rights has existed in one form or another since earliest times. In 1948 the United Nations pulled together much of the thinking in this area and issued the Universal Declaration of Human Rights. Contained within this were the rights that were deemed necessary for human beings to live a decent life. The rights inherent within assertion training are in line with many of these basic human rights.

GENERAL RIGHTS

While there is no definitive list of these assertive rights, many people agree that the following general rights could be included. So if you wish to behave assertively in many situations in your life then you need to accept that you have the right to:

- Your own opinions, views and ideas (which may or may not be different from other people's)
- A fair hearing for these opinions, views and ideas
- Have needs and wants that may be different from other people's
- *Ask* (not demand) that others respond to your needs and wants
- Refuse a request without feeling guilty or selfish
- Have feelings and to express them assertively if you so choose
- Be 'human', e.g. to be wrong sometimes
- Decide not to assert yourself (e.g. to choose not to raise a particular issue)
- Be your own self: this may be the same as, or different from, what others would like you to be (it includes choosing friends, interests etc.)
- Have others respect your rights

JOB RIGHTS

When you apply the idea of rights to your job you can probably see that some of them will be spelt out clearly (written down in some cases), while others will be less clear and not written down. In the first category will be your rights in such areas as:

- Contract of employment
- Working conditions
- Maternity leave
- Redundancy payment

Such rights are enshrined in the law of the land. You may not be clear about the details of such rights. However, you are aware you have rights in these areas and if you suspect they are being violated, then you can find out the detail from the appropriate source.

Also falling into the first category are the rights that you have, which are a result of the policies of the organization you work for. Some organizations do more than meet the minimum legal requirements in aspects such as redundancy or holidays; their policies give employees additional rights. In addition, some organizations develop policies not covered by government legislation, for example:

- The right to an appraisal of job performance at least once a year
- The right to a certain amount of time off in lieu
- The right to study for certain recognized qualifications in company time without loss of pay

Again, you may not be clear on the details of these rights but you know where you can get such details, as they are probably written down somewhere.

Even where the above rights are clear, it still leaves a large area of activity in your job where the rights are not clearly spelt out. In our different ways, we set out to reduce the degree of uncertainty that results from this. Some people work on the basis of the less said the better, as that gives them, as they see it, maximum room for manoeuvre. Others set about clarifying the rights they would like. This process can start early on when taking a new job. You will ask your manager questions to clarify what your rights are (though you probably won't use the word rights). Together you clarify the position. In some cases, it may be useful to refer to a job description, which may clarify such things as the level of expenditure you have the right to authorize.

The process of clarifying rights is helped if you have a picture in your mind of the rights you would like to have. You can then test these out on the persons that you work with and for. Some of them may be readily agreed by the other person, others may need further discussion and modification.

The list below may be helpful in getting you started:

- The right to be clear on what is expected of me
- The right to know how my manager sees my performance
- The right to get on with my job in my own way once objectives and constraints have been agreed
- The right to make mistakes from time to time
- The right to have a say/veto in selecting the people who work for me
- The right to expect work of a certain standard from my staff
- The right to criticize the performance of a member of staff when it falls below the required standard
- The right to be consulted about decisions that affect me
- The right to take decisions about matters that affect my department or area of work
- The right to refuse certain requests

The last right sometimes gives rise to difficulty, particularly where it concerns you and your manager. In accepting a job and signing a contract of employment you may have relinquished certain rights. Included within this would be the right to refuse a request from your manager (assuming it is legal and part of your job). In this case, although you do not have the right to refuse, you do have the right to state your position and any problem that the request may cause for you. With requests from colleagues and staff you are much more likely to have the right to refuse.

Accepting rights

Now, it is one thing to *understand* the above rights and even to *agree* that they are your rights. But this does not necessarily mean that you will act upon those rights. In order for you to *act* upon your rights you need to really *accept* them.

Y ou can test whether you really accept a particular right by asking yourself:

- 'Do I drop my assertiveness at any early sign of resistance?'
- 'After an assertion do I feel guilt or regret, or do I wonder if I did the right thing?'
- 'How often do I have to keep reminding myself I have this right?'
- 'Do I have to steel myself to exercise this right?'

You may find it useful at this point to go back through the list of general rights and identify which of these rights, if any, you have difficulty in accepting. Remember, accepting means being willing to stand up for them in the face of resistance from others. For those you have difficulty in accepting ask yourself:

- 'What are the effects on my work, social life and relations with others, as a result of me not accepting this right?'

Having answered this question, you can sometimes move towards accepting the right by repeating to yourself 'I do have the right to ... '.

Later on in this chapter we look in more detail at how the beliefs you hold may make it difficult for you to make the change at this level. However, before moving onto this we would like to consider the issue of responsibilities.

Responsibilities

Concentrating upon rights as we have done so far can give you the impression that assertion is a bit one way i.e. you exercising your rights without sufficient attention being paid to other people's rights. When this occurs it can contribute to the confusion that exists in some people's minds between assertion and aggression. A way of ensuring that this does not happen is for you to accept the responsibilities that go with rights. Table 3.1 gives some suggestions for responsibilities that accompany some of the job rights we mentioned earlier. If you fail to accept these responsibilities it makes it more difficult for other people to accept that you have the rights in the first place.

Table 3.1   Rights and responsibilities

Rights	Responsibilities
• To be allowed to get on with your job in your own way once objectives and constraints have been clarified	• To abide by these constraints • To use your time productively in working towards these objectives
• To have a say in selecting the people who are to work for you	• Not to abuse this right for personal ends (e.g. vetoing a person whom you see as a threat to you in your job)
• To make a mistake from time to time	• To acknowledge a mistake rather than blaming others • To put it right • To learn from it, i.e. not repeat it
• To expect work of a certain standard from the people working for you	• To let people know what the standards are
• To criticize the performance of your staff when it falls below this standard	• To do it assertively • To recognize there may be legitimate reasons for this

OVERRIDING RESPONSIBILITIES

If you want to stand up for your rights *assertively*, then you have the responsibility to:

- Accept and respect the rights of others. It would be easy to become so concerned about your own rights that you lose sight of other people's. If you have the right to make a mistake from time to time so do others
- Be selective about the rights you stand up for and when. Sticking rigidly to what you believe your rights to be, or taking a stand every time a right is infringed however slightly, can be counter-productive

Beliefs

We said at the beginning of this chapter that an important factor in determining the rights you feel able to accept or give to others, is the beliefs you hold. Before looking at this relationship, let us define what we mean by beliefs.

WHAT ARE BELIEFS?

Beliefs are views/opinions/statements that we hold to be true about ourselves, other people, ideas or situations. They are things about which we *feel emotionally certain*. For example:

- 'I believe my ideas are as good as other people's'
- 'I believe that people can change, if they want to'

The beliefs you hold about yourself can:

- Be about *who you are*, e.g. 'I am a practical person'; 'I am an extrovert'
- *Prevent you* from doing things, e.g. 'I can't handle aggressive people'; 'I mustn't tell people what I really think'
- *Compel you* to do things, e.g. 'I must always be at my best'; 'I should give as good as I get'

HOW DO BELIEFS AFFECT BEHAVIOUR?

The pattern can be seen in Figure 3.1. So, for example, if you believe that your ideas are not as good as other people's, then you will find it difficult to accept the right to express your ideas and to have a fair hearing for them. This in turn means that you are likely to behave nonassertively in a range of situations by, for instance, in a meeting, holding back on your ideas or putting them forward in a tentative way. The result is, not surprisingly, that you fail to influence other people in the meeting. This affects your beliefs in the sense that it reinforces your specific belief that your ideas are not very good. The circle continues in that it is now even more difficult for you to accept the rights mentioned above.

The picture is complicated by the way we interpret the situations we are involved in. The result in this example may be for you reasonably clear cut in the sense that you can see no evidence of your ideas being incorporated into

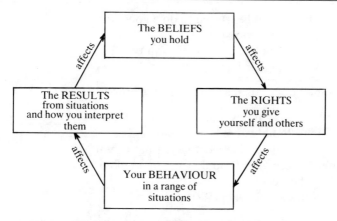

Figure 3.1   How do beliefs affect behaviour?

the outcome of the meeting. In other situations it may be nothing like as clear-cut and different interpretations can be put upon the results. Your interpretation will be highly influenced by the beliefs you bring to the situation. So if you believe that you are not very influential then you look for evidence to support that belief. And of course, you can find examples where you failed to influence someone. You do not spend time looking for examples of where you did influence. So your interpretation was that you were not influential. The convenience of this is that it confirms your belief in the first place that you are not influential. Even where there is a clear-cut example of you being influential, there is a danger that you rationalize it away by saying something like 'Oh well, that was the exception that proved the rule'.

So our beliefs influence not just our behaviour but also the way we interpret the results that follow from our behaviour. They become our filter on the world, so that we seek out things that reinforce our beliefs and ignore or explain away things that do not fit our beliefs. If all this sounds rather bad news, the good news is that you can do something about your beliefs, thereby helping you to break out of what can become a self-fulfilling spiral. For you to do this you need firstly to become aware of the sort of beliefs that tend to lead to this pattern, and to nonassertive and aggressive behaviour. We call them:

BARRIER BELIEFS
These are beliefs that act as a barrier to you behaving assertively. Some examples that lead to aggressive behaviour are:

- Attack is the best form of defence
- Aggression gets results

- Other people cannot be trusted to do a good job
- I am superior, I know best
- Other people should stand on their own two feet
- I must give as good as I get

Some examples of beliefs that lead to nonassertion are:

- I am not as important as others
- My opinions do not count
- Other people will not like me if I say what I think
- It is safer to keep your head down in times of conflict
- I should put others first
- I must get this absolutely perfect

One of the characteristics of these barrier beliefs is that they restrict you in the way you behave and reduce your opportunities for learning. So we see it as important to modify these barrier beliefs into assertive ones.

ASSERTIVE BELIEFS

These beliefs increase your chances to learn through using assertive behaviour. Some examples of such beliefs are:

- I am responsible for what happens to me
- I am in control, I can choose how to behave
- I can change
- I can initiate actions to achieve results
- I can learn from feedback
- I believe assertiveness does work

The question is how do you modify some of these barrier beliefs into assertive ones.

MODIFYING BELIEFS

Firstly it is useful to get clear what your barrier beliefs are and then to decide upon one that you would like to change. This is a useful process in its own right as you may not be consciously aware of these beliefs. Some of the ways of changing a barrier belief into an assertive one are given below.

1. Contrast the belief with the knowledge you now have

Beliefs are formed as a result of the experiences you have. These experiences may be significant one-offs or less significant ones repeated regularly. They may date from early childhood and continue through education and work. The point is that a belief may be dated in the sense that what you know now may be different from what you knew when the belief was formed. However, you may not have updated the belief in the light of this new knowledge.

An example would be if you formed a belief at school that you were 'thick' because you needed to ask questions. The teacher who instilled this belief, was at the time a powerful figure to you. However, looking back with the knowledge you now have, that asking questions is crucial for learning and contributing, you can see now that the teacher was not a good teacher if he or she instilled this belief. However, the belief may still be influencing your behaviour at meetings.

2. Knowing what other people believe

Particularly where you respect another person, finding out what this person believes, for example about getting results, can lead you to modify your own belief in that area. This process is more likely to occur if you can personally discuss with this person how the belief works for him or her.

3. Looking for instances that disprove the belief

Earlier we described how beliefs can lead you to filter out examples that do not fit in with your belief. This approach encourages you to put your energy into identifying just such examples. So if you want to modify a belief that you do not have much to contribute, focus in on those instances where you do say something, rather than when you do not. At this stage do not concern yourself overmuch with the quality of what you say.

4. Acting 'as if' you held a different belief

This is a particularly powerful way to modify a belief and is one of the main methods we use on our training courses. So you focus on the assertive belief you want to hold and then identify:

- The different rights you would give yourself if you did hold this belief
- In what situations and with whom you would want to hold this belief?
- What specific assertive behaviours you would use in handling these situations and people?
- What would be the pay-offs or rewards for you in using these behaviours?

Finally you go at risk and use the behaviours you have identified. There is a good chance you will experience positive results. This serves to weaken the barrier belief and to strengthen the belief you have 'tried on'.

Summary

In this chapter we have stepped back from assertive behaviour to look at the issues of rights and beliefs. We have said that:

- Being clear on, and accepting your rights and other people's rights, provides you with a basis for assertive behaviour

- Accepting the responsibilities that go with your rights helps to ensure you behave assertively, and not aggressively
- The beliefs you hold are your filter on the world
- You can modify those barrier beliefs that work against your behaving assertively

4. Starting to be more assertive

In preceding chapters we have dealt with some of the concepts of assertiveness, begun to recognize assertive, aggressive and nonassertive behaviours, and identified your rights within assertiveness. In this chapter we begin the practical process of helping you to behave more assertively at work.

We believe that any skill, whether it be playing golf, public speaking, or interacting with others, can best be developed through practising. This is equally true of assertiveness. So, to start the practice we have chosen a number of situations that people have to handle at work. The situations are ones in which you might sometimes find yourself behaving aggressively or nonassertively. They occur fairly often, so there is usually plenty of opportunity to practise them. They are mostly short interactions with fairly straightforward outcomes, making them an ideal starting point for improving assertiveness. With each of the situations we give a number of hints for behaving assertively in them.

The situations we will be dealing with are: making requests, refusing requests, disagreeing and stating your views, giving and receiving praise, and giving bad news. For each of these situations we look at the beliefs people often hold (including the rights they think they have) which can lead to nonassertive or aggressive behaviour. We then give hints for behaving assertively in each of the situations.

Situation 1. Making requests

Do you sometimes find it difficult to make requests of other people at work, or are you very tentative or abrupt when doing so? Sometimes it is easier to make a request according to whom you are asking. So you might find it easier, say, to ask a colleague than to ask a member of staff or a superior. Typical requests might be: asking a colleague for a report earlier than usual, asking a manager for a change of responsibilities, asking a member of staff to work an extra weekend shift. If you are not able to make requests assertively, you can often end up missing opportunities, not taking initiatives, and not getting the best use out of available resources; alternatively, you might cause others to be resentful and uncooperative.

Any difficulties you might experience probably stem from the *beliefs* you hold about making requests. These may include:

- I'll put other people in a position where they can't refuse
- If people refuse it means they don't like me
- It's a sign of weakness to ask for things
- My needs are not that important/not as important as other people's
- If people do things for me it will put me under an obligation to them
- I have no right to ask

If you hold the above beliefs then it is likely that you will avoid making requests or you will make them apologetically. That is to say, you will act *nonassertively*.

In contrast, your beliefs may include:

- Others have no right to refuse
- A refusal constitutes an attack upon me personally
- My needs are more important than other people's
- Other people ought to be pleased to help me out

Then you will be hostile or demanding when making the request. The unspoken challenge indicated by your tone of voice is, 'Refuse if you dare!' With all of these you will be behaving *aggressively*.

It is realistic to expect that you will need to make requests of other people as part of your job. Some of these requests may well be for people to 'go beyond their call of duty'. We refer to both these as work requests. In addition, there will be times when you want to make other requests of someone, for example for a lift home, or to go for a drink at lunchtime. These we call personal requests. With all the requests the key to behaving assertively is to believe that *you have the right to ask, the other person has the right to be asked in an assertive way, and the right to refuse.* With this last right there are sometimes exceptions, so that a person may not always have the right to refuse. For instance, in accepting a contract of employment for a particular job a person may have *relinquished* their right to refuse work at certain times or in certain circumstances. Even so, *they still have the right to state any problems that the request will cause them.*

By the way, we make no distinctions between reasonable or unreasonable requests, largely because this can only be a subjective judgement anyway. Second, 'unreasonable' can be an emotive word, pushing you into responding with aggression. If you accept the assertive rights for both parties mentioned above, then the issue of reasonable versus unreasonable has less significance.

HINTS FOR MAKING REQUESTS
The aim is to make requests in a straightforward, open way; *not* to make it difficult for the other person to refuse.

Don't apologize profusely. For instance, 'I'm very sorry to bother you, I hope you don't mind ...' or 'I hope you won't think I'm a nuisance, but do you think you could possibly ...'.

Be direct. For example, speaking to a colleague: 'Anne, I'd really like the report on the Harrison project by the end of next week. Can that be done?' If you make hints rather than requests people will either become suspicious or impatient or both, and say to themselves 'Why doesn't he get straight to the point?'

Keep it short. Long-winded explanations get confusing and increase the chances that you will start justifying yourself.

Don't justify yourself for making the request; e.g. 'I wouldn't normally ask anybody. I don't like to be a nuisance, but the car's broken down and the neighbour's in bed with flu.'

Give a reason for your request, if you think it will help, but be sure it's genuine and keep it brief. 'Pete, I shall be without the car tomorrow; would you be able to give me a lift?' or 'Alan , I need the figures for the meeting next week; will you be able to let me have yours by Friday?'

Don't 'sell' your request with flattery or tempting benefits: 'Linda, you're *just* the person, would you ...' or 'Bob, I'm sure this will interest you, ...'.

Don't play on people's friendship or good nature: 'Be a pal and get this to me by dinner time' or 'It would be really kind of you if you could ...'.

Don't take a refusal personally, even when the request is of a more personal nature, or when the colleague is also a friend. Otherwise, they might end up feeling guilty about refusing.

Respect the other person's right to say no. With a personal request, take 'No' for an answer. Don't become persistent with nonassertive pleading or aggressive bullying. With a work request, give more information and clarification, find out why the person is unable to meet your request. If the answer is still 'No', put your energy into joint problem-solving rather than into necessarily persuading the other person to meet your request as originally outlined. (For further explanation of this see Chapter 11.)

Situation 2. Refusing requests

A frequent experience for many managers and specialists is that, when faced with a request at work, they find it difficult to say 'No', or their 'No' comes across like a hammer blow. As with making requests, any difficulties you may have often stem from the *beliefs* you hold. These could include things like:

- Others will feel angry/hurt if I refuse
- They'll cease to like me
- It's rude/selfish to refuse
- I have no right to refuse
- If I refuse, I relinquish the right to make requests of others
- Their needs are more important than mine

These beliefs will lead you to say 'Yes' when you really want to say 'No', to feel guilty about saying 'No', or to give excuses (instead of the real reason) for not agreeing to the request. An example of this last one would be saying; 'I can't take on the survey at the moment, I haven't got time', when the real reason is you do not think the survey is of value. All of this is behaving *nonassertively*.

Later on, after having said 'Yes' when you really wanted to say 'No', you might find you have taken on more work than you can handle. You can also start to feel resentful that you, or others, are doing things you are far from happy about. You may even take this resentment out on the person who made the request, whereas in fact you are angry at yourself for not saying 'No'.

In contrast to the above beliefs, you might *believe* that:

- Others have no right to make such requests of you
- Other people ought to sort themselves out
- If I meet their requests people will soon get the idea I'm a 'soft touch'

These beliefs will result in responses like 'Not likely, you've got a nerve' or, 'Why ask me all the time?' which are examples of *aggressively* refusing a request.

The key to refusing assertively is to believe that *other people have the right to ask; you have the right to refuse*. Where the definition of the job limits your right to refuse, remember *you still have the right to state the difficulties the request will cause*.

HINTS FOR REFUSING REQUESTS ASSERTIVELY

Keep the reply short but not abrupt, avoiding long rambling justifications along the lines of: 'I wouldn't normally say no, only ... you know how it is, I hope you don't mind.'

Simply say: 'I prefer not to ... ', or 'I'd rather not ... ', or 'No, I don't want to ... ', or 'I'm not happy to ... '. These phrases are particularly useful for refusing personal requests.

Give the real reason for refusing; do not invent an excuse. To check whether it is an excuse, ask yourself the question: 'If I could get around this problem, would I then be happy to say "Yes"?' If you still would not be happy to agree to the request then you have an excuse not the real reason.

Avoid 'I can't' phrases because they easily start sounding like excuses.

Don't apologize profusely: 'I'm terribly sorry ... do you mind very much if ...?'.

Acknowledge the requester when she has invited you to do something or when she has taken an unusual initiative for her: 'Thank you, Anne, but I'm not ready to take my lunch break yet', or 'I'm certainly interested in the meetings, Pat, however ... '.

Identify yourself with your decision rather than hiding behind rules, precedents and third parties: 'I'm not prepared to bend the rules on this', or 'I don't want to change the ... ' (rather than: 'Senior management wouldn't agree to change the ... ').

Ask for clarification or more information, such as 'What detail does the survey need to go in to?', or 'Do you need it by Friday morning or later in the afternoon?'

Ask for more time to decide on the request, for instance if you want to check workloads. However, do not use this as a tactic to delay the inevitable.

Nonverbal behaviour. Especially with short replies you need to slow down, speak steadily and with warmth, otherwise replies like 'No, I don't want to' can sound abrupt.

IF THE REQUESTER BECOMES PERSISTENT

Often people ignore your right to refuse, and they become persistent in making their request. We are not so much thinking of people asking for more information or clarification when you refuse, but of people using ploys like the following to get you to change your mind:

- Questioning your judgement: 'Are you sure about that?'
- Nonassertive pleading; 'It wouldn't half, um ... get me out of a hole if you ...'
- Aggressive (sometimes 'fatherly') bullying: 'Oh go on. I'm sure you can!'
- Blaming you: 'You'll leave me with a terrible problem'
- Quoting precedent: 'But you did it for us last time'

When people become persistent we suggest the following:

Repeat your refusal adding the reason if you didn't give it first time. Leave out the reason if you outlined the reason fully first time. Slow down and emphasize any words you are repeating.

Don't search for 'better' reasons. You will probably only come up with flimsy excuses that the requester will either propose 'solutions' to or dismiss altogether. This example demonstrates what can often happen:

Initial assertive refusal	'I don't want to involve Laura in the annual schedule as I've already agreed with her that she won't be involved this year.'
Persistence	'It wouldn't be difficult to tell her you've changed your mind.'
Excuse	'Well, anyway she's got a lot on at the moment with the Coates job.'
Persistence	'I'll get one of my people to give her a hand on that one, that'll give her time for the schedule.'

49

As soon as you put forward excuses you are making life difficult for yourself. So after the first persistent statement it would have been more assertive and effective to have said: 'No, I *prefer* to stick to my agreement with Laura.' If you inadvertently give an excuse, then retrieve the situation by 'coming clean' with the real reason as soon as you can.

Situation 3. Disagreeing and stating your views

At work and in your social life you experience different events from other people; even with the same event you might experience it in different ways. All this leads you, quite legitimately, to see things from your own point of view. This will sometimes be the same as other people's, sometimes different. You probably exchange these points of view when you meet. This can either be in casual encounters, where viewpoints are aired more or less as an end in themselves or it can be in more formal meetings, where disagreeing and stating views is part of the larger processes of decision making and problem solving. Unfortunately, both casual encounters and more formal meetings can at times resemble a 'battle of wits', with enormous energy going into 'point scoring', rather like a debating society; or else they adopt a cocktail party atmosphere, where the game is to change your mind as soon as anybody disagrees with you. The following exchange illustrates both point scoring and changing your mind.

The situation is that a new system for budget returns has been in trial operation for a month. This is being reviewed in a meeting:

DAVE: 'I reckon the old procedure's a real improvement.
The old one never worked properly.'
COLIN: 'That's not true. The old one was far better. This
new one takes too long to fill in, for a start. It wants
scrapping altogether.'
LIZ: 'It's all right if you know what you're doing.'   (*Point scoring*)
COLIN: 'On the contrary, it's all right if you've got plenty   (*Point scoring*)
of time to spare.'
DAVE: 'Well, I suppose it is a bit time consuming in some   (*Change of mind*)
ways.'

In this exchange there is no attempt to recognize each other's position. In fact, all the points of view are valid, in that, while the new system may not work for Colin, it may well work for Liz and Dave. The likely outcome of the exchange is that, whatever system is adopted, it will meet the needs of one, maybe two, people but not all. A more useful outcome would be a system that meets the needs of all parties. But to achieve that kind of outcome the behaviour would need to be assertive, instead of as it was—mainly aggressive, with some nonassertion.

So, *aggressive behaviour* often stokes up conflict by emphasizing disagreement and down-playing agreement. It tends to dismiss the other person's ideas and opinions as worthless, to state opinions as facts, and to take up an entrenched position. It puts down the other person either through sarcasm or direct hostility. It uses statements like:

- 'Nonsense, that won't work'
- 'You don't know what you're talking about'
- 'That will just cause problems'
- 'That machine is a complete waste of time'
- 'Another of your time-saving ideas, would you say?'
- 'I don't care what you say, I'm sticking to ...'
  Aggressive behaviour stems from *beliefs* along the lines of:
- Things are always black and white; there are no grey areas
- Other people can only be right if I'm wrong: both parties can't be right
- I'm more vulnerable if I'm seen to be wrong
- It will show weakness if I change my mind
- Other people have no right to disagree with me

The immediate result of people disagreeing and stating their views *aggressively* is that the issues can get forgotten as the emotions start to take over. Thus, new facts, valid viewpoints, and potentially useful ideas get lost. In turn, this means that the eventual outcomes, such as solutions and decisions, are not as effective as they could be.

Nonassertive behaviour dismisses your own ideas and opinions as being worthless or less important than those of other people. It seeks to avoid open conflict by glossing over any disagreements that exist and by changing tack in the face of other people's challenges. It expresses disagreement and viewpoints tentatively or apologetically, if at all. It may sometimes involve keeping quiet about doubts altogether or airing them afterwards to different people. It consists of statements like:

- 'Mmm, I suppose you're right, ... really'
- 'Er, ... I'm not sure I can agree there'
- 'I don't like to disagree but, ... um, ... have you. ...?'
- 'Oh, ... really? ... well ... maybe I've got the wrong impression'

It arises out of *beliefs* that include:

- Disagreeing always leads to conflict, which is unpleasant
- People will think I'm just being awkward if I raise doubts
- Other people will always be upset or annoyed if I disagree
- If I state my point of view I stand the risk of being wrong/ridiculed, etc
- Both parties can't be right
- I'm usually wrong anyway
- I don't have the right to disagree

The immediate result of being nonassertive about disagreeing and stating views is that some quite valid difficulties are not raised and are therefore not taken into account in any eventual solutions. Also, decisions can be taken to which you are not fully committed. Other people will be understandably irritated when you admit later on: 'Well, I didn't really agree with it at the time but I didn't like to say so.'

Assertive behaviour involves disagreeing and agreeing openly and stating your viewpoints clearly and firmly. It means that you do not put yourself or others down. It comes from *beliefs* such as:

- I and others have the right to have opinions and for these to be different
- I and others have the right to state opinions and to disagree
- Disagreements do not necessarily lead to conflict
- Opinions are not necessarily right and wrong, merely different

HINTS FOR DISAGREEING AND STATING YOUR VIEWS ASSERTIVELY

State disagreement clearly: 'I don't go along with ... ', 'My experience is different in that ... ', 'I see it differently in that ... '.

Express doubts in a constructive way: 'Will that lead to X?' or 'I see a difficulty in that.... Can we get round it?' rather than knocking people's ideas down like skittles: 'That won't work' or 'That will cause Y'.

Use 'I' statements to distinguish your opinion from fact and to distinguish your experience from that of other people:

- 'As I see it, ...'
- 'I believe ...'
- 'I find that ...'
- 'My experience is ...'

Change your opinion in the light of new information (rather than as a result of emotional behaviour from other people) and be firm and honest about doing so: 'In the light of ... I now think ...'.

Give reasons for your disagreement if you think it will lead to more progress. 'I don't agree with X because of the effect it has on Y.'

State what parts you agree and disagree with: 'I don't agree that the procedure affects *all* departments in that way' or 'I agree that we need to change, but not as quickly as you suggest.'

Recognize other people's point of view. 'I appreciate that you see it differently from me.; 'I recognize that it affects you differently.'

The result of disagreeing and stating your views assertively is that information, viewpoints, and ideas do not get lost; issues are not avoided or 'fudged'. It increases the chances that further down the track people will be able to come up with mutually acceptable solutions.

52

Situation 4. Giving praise

We often hear managers say things like 'You only hear from Dave when something goes wrong'. It is quite common for people to be working in an environment where praise is rare, and where the recipient of the rare morsel thinks suspiciously, 'What's he after now?' There are a number of reasons why you might not give praise, including your *beliefs* about giving praise, such as:

- It's soft or soggy to give praise
- If I praise them they'll start relaxing (the standards)
- They're only doing what they're paid for
- They'll think I want something
- People will only learn to do better if you point out their mistakes, so praise doesn't serve any useful purpose

In addition, you might be reluctant to give praise because your *experiences* of giving praise in the past have been unrewarding; maybe:

- You felt uncomfortable or embarrassed
- You couldn't find the right words
- The praise turned 'sour' on you
- It was not well received

All this means that now you might behave *nonassertively*, and either avoid giving praise altogether, or else give praise:

- Apologetically: 'I hope you won't mind my saying so, but I really thought you handled that customer well'
- Hesitantly, so it comes across less sincerely: 'Sylvia , I liked . . . er, I mean I thought your report was really very good'
- And at the same time put yourself down; 'Pat, I thought your presentation was good. I wish mine were as good as that'

Alternatively, you might behave *aggressively*, in that you give the praise:

- Grudgingly: 'Well, that wasn't a bad effort for you, Jim'; or 'You did it well, in the end.' Here you are giving and taking back at the same time
- With double meaning: 'That was an interesting presentation, John. Did Sue help you prepare it?' The intention is to praise, but the implication is that John couldn't have produced it on his own
- Gushingly: 'That was absolutely splendid, Jones. I thought you did a really magnificent job. Well done! Keep up the good work.' So either the praise comes over as insincere or you end up patronizing the other person—treating them as a father might treat a child

53

Note

Sometimes people use sarcasm: 'That was really *some* report.' This is usually not praise but criticism disguised as praise.

If you are unable to give praise assertively you leave people trying to guess whether the work they do meets your expectations, or making assumptions along the lines of 'no news is good news.'

Assertive behaviour involves expressing thoughts, feelings, beliefs and wants in direct, honest and appropriate ways. Because of the interchange of ideas and resources that occurs between people at work, it is inevitable that there will be times when you want to acknowledge someone for what they have done or said. This person may be a colleague, a member of staff, or a senior manager; or even a client or supplier. In addition to showing acknowledgement, praise also has a *learning function*. People learn not only from mistakes but also from successes. So praise, especially very specific praise, gives the other person a picture of your standards and informs them when they have achieved them.

HINTS FOR GIVING PRAISE

Maintain eye contact, but in a relaxed way: not looking as though embarrassed to give praise, but not staring the person down.

Keep the praise brief and clear, avoiding extra phrases to pad it out and make it more 'comfortable'.

Use 'I' statements along the lines of 'I like the report on ...'; 'I'm pleased with the way you handled the visit, Dave.'

Make it specific to detailed aspects of the work wherever possible. 'I liked the report on ... I particularly thought it was a good idea to have the summary at the beginning.'

Specific statements like the last one give people information about what would be useful to repeat in future. They also increase the chances of the praise being seen as sincere.

Situation 5. Receiving praise

All too often you might feel uncomfortable or foolish when you are on the receiving end of praise. This is often because, from your culture or upbringing, you have come to hold certain *beliefs* about receiving praise. For instance:

- It's impolite/boastful to agree with praise
- Accepting praise means being obligated/grateful to someone

So you fall into one of the following traps:

Behaving nonassertively

- Shrugging off the praise: 'Oh, it was nothing, really it wasn't'
- Giving praise in return: 'Er, I think your last report was good as well'
- Putting yourself down: 'Well, I'm not really very good. Sue's brilliant at organizing these studies'

Behaving aggressively

- Challenging the person's judgement: 'You thought that was good? I thought it was second rate, myself'
- Boastfulness: 'Well, of course it was. I always make a good presentation'

Both the nonassertive and the aggressive responses above discount the praise. They thus reduce the chances that the giver will want to repeat the experience.

HINTS FOR RECEIVING PRAISE ASSERTIVELY

Simply thank the giver: 'Thanks, Dave.'

Keep your response short: 'Thanks, Dave, I'm glad you liked it.'

Agree with or accept the praise: 'Thanks, Liz, I thought the presentation went well'; or 'Thank you Liz, I was pleased with the way it went'. If you also like something it is assertive to say so.

Note

If you disagree with the praise certainly qualify your reply, but still thank the giver.

Situation 6. Giving bad news

From time to time we have to pass on information or a decision that we feel pretty sure the other person is not going to like! We refer to this as giving 'bad news', for example:

- Telling a colleague that the report you are doing for her will not be ready on time
- Telling a member of staff that he isn't going to get the regrading/ promotion he was expecting
- Telling your staff about changes in company policy that affect them

These and similar situations can give rise to problems, especially when the bad news clashes with the other person's *expectations*. These expectations may be based on personal preferences, on custom and practice, on current company policy or on a specific agreement. Indeed, you may even have fuelled these expectations by your own *previous nonassertion*! For example, by:

55

- Not mentioning a particular item
- Not responding to or clarifying something the other person has said
- Hinting or leading the person to believe that something was possible when it was not ('I'll see what I can do')

When you give 'bad news' to others it's possible to behave *nonassertively*, by:

- Procrastinating ('I really haven't got time to do it at the moment')
- Being over-apologetic (maybe to avoid criticism)
- Being the 'good guy' by blaming or hiding behind other people or the organization ('If it was left to me you'd be top priority')
- Dressing up the 'bad news' to such an extent that it no longer gives an accurate picture of the decision or information

Alternatively you may behave *aggressively*, dismissing the other person with phrases like:

- 'Well there it is, nothing you can do about it!'
- 'Hard luck! Don't blame me!'
- 'You'll just have to manage without'

The *aim* in giving bad news is to pass on the information or decision acurately and in a way that does not further undermine the confidence/morale/motivation of the other person.

You are more likely to achieve this aim if you behaved *assertively*. So first of all you need to accept that:

- You have the *right* to inform the other person of changes
- The other person has the *right* to be kept informed and to know the reasons behind the changes

HINTS FOR GIVING BAD NEWS

Take the initiative in passing on the 'bad news', (if you speak to the other person rather than waiting for them to find out, you are in a better position to have prepared and to handle it assertively).

Introduce the topic, and if appropriate refer to previous agreement/arrangement/policy.

Give the specific 'bad news':

- State what has happened/changed: 'The position now is that ...'; 'I/we won't be able to ...'; 'You will now be ... instead of ...'
- Give only brief reasons/background at this stage (better to expand later as necessary, rather than get into details too early)
- Explain clearly what actions, if any, you have taken/propose to take
- Keep it brief without being abrupt
- Keep it factual in content and tone of voice
- Maintain eye contact (if face to face interaction)

Indicate any implications for the other person, or any advantages for them or the company that follow from the changes.

Agree to listen to suggestions for overcoming any problems they foresee, but don't make promises you'll find difficult to keep.

Throughout the interaction use 'I' statements to emphasize that you take responsibility for the 'bad news'.

- Don't hide behind the organization/other people, e.g. 'The company, in its wisdom have decided to . . .'; 'Those clowns in personnel have come up with another earth-shattering scheme'

One of the most difficult situations for many people is when they are passing on bad news that they do not personally agree with. If you find yourself in this situation we suggest you:

- Make your position clear to the decision maker or your immediate manager at the time you find out about the bad news
- Decide whether you are going to make your position clear to the person to whom you are passing on the bad news. You may choose to do this if you feel your credibility would be undermined by you failing to make your own view clear

You have the right to have your own views about the 'bad news'. However, you also have a responsibility to pass it on in a way that does not undermine the decision or proposed changes. So you can say something like: 'I don't personally agree that this is the best way forward and I have made my views clear to my manager. However, the decision has been taken and I would like to find ways of making it work.'

Where you don't have the initiative—first check out the person's understanding of the 'bad news' before following any of the above hints.

Summary

The six situations we have dealt with provide a useful starting point in behaving more assertively, as they do not usually require long or complex assertions. However, handling them more successfully can give a big return for the time invested.

In Chapter 7 we look at the other side of the coin to 'giving and receiving praise', which is 'giving and receiving criticism'. This is more complicated and is best dealt with after reading the next two chapters.

5. Types of assertion

We have talked so far of three types of behaviour: ass, agg, and na. Already you may have realized that these are umbrella categories, covering a range of behaviours. So there are different types of assertion, just as there are different types of na and agg. In this chapter we introduce six different types of assertion and give some guidelines on when and how to use them. At the end of the chapter, there is a short recognition test to help you identify the different types.

We suggest you regard these types as some of the options you have available within the spectrum of assertiveness. Some of them you will use already, perhaps in a slightly different format. Being able to use all the types gives you a greater repertoire of behaviours for handling the wide range of situations you encounter. In future chapters (such as Chapter 9, 'Handling aggression from others') we will build these types into strategies for dealing with specific situations.

Six types of assertion

There are several types of assertion, but the ones we find useful are:

Basic	Negative feelings
Empathetic	Consequence
Discrepancy	Responsive

We will go on to give definitions and examples for each of these types, so that you can distinguish them.

BASIC ASSERTION

This is a straightforward statement where you stand up for your rights. It involves making clear your needs, wants, beliefs, opinions, or feelings. Examples of basic assertion are:

- 'As I see it, the system is working well'
- 'I would like to make some changes to ... '
- 'I need to be away by 5 o'clock'
- 'The cost is £2000'
- 'I feel very pleased with the way the issue has been resolved'

When to use basic assertion

This is the most common form of assertion, which you use everyday to make your needs, wants, and opinions known. In addition, you use it to give praise or compliments, information, and facts to others. It is particularly appropriate to use it when you are raising an issue with someone for the first time. So, for instance, it would be the starting point for your discussion with your manager over a regrading of your job. You might say: 'Doug, I'd like to talk about regrading my job. Now as I see it, (state the position) ... So what I'd like to happen is ... (state your suggestion).' All these are basic assertions.

You can also repeat a basic assertion to re-emphasize your needs and wants, when you feel that your initial statement of them is being ignored or played down.

This assertion contains the element of empathy as well as a statement of your needs or wants. By empathy we mean the ability to put yourself in the other person's position and recognize the feelings, needs, and wants that they may have. Some examples of empathetic assertion are:

- 'I appreciate that you don't like the new procedure, Jenny. However, until it's changed I'd like you to keep your people working to it'
- 'I know you're busy at the moment, John. However, I'd like to make a quick request of you'
- 'I recognize that it's difficult to be precise on costs at this stage. However, it would be helpful if you'd give me a rough estimate'

As you see from these examples, empathy is different from sympathy, although the two are sometimes confused. Sympathy usually involves feeling sorry for someone, and leaves people where they are—feeling sorry for themselves. This works against your behaving assertively towards them. For instance: 'What a shame you didn't get that job. I know you must be feeling very disappointed. Ah well ... there we are.' By contrast, empathy gives due recognition for where people are, and also moves them or you forward: 'I recognize that you're very disappointed about not getting that job ... I think there will be other opportunities.'

When to use empathetic assertion
Empathetic assertion can be used when the other person is engrossed in a situation and you want to indicate that you are aware of and sensitive to their situation. So acknowledging that someone is busy, has a different opinion than you, or feels particularly strongly about an issue shows that you recognize their position. This enables the other person to realize that you are not dismissing them, which in turn increases the chances that they will recognize your position and respond assertively. Empathy is an essential ingredient for resolving conflicts in which people are behaving aggressively. (We refer to this in Chapter 9.)

Empathetic assertion is also useful in holding you back from over-reacting

59

with aggression. This is roughly how it works. With empathy you have to give yourself time to imagine the other person's position, so automatically you slow down your response to them. When this happens you are less likely to see them as an aggressive person who is personally stopping your needs from being met. You can then go on and behave assertively towards them.

Empathetic assertion can be powerful behaviour, so it is important not to use it as a means of getting your own needs met at the expense of the other person's. It is easy to over-use phrases like 'I appreciate your feelings on this, but ... ' so that the currency of empathy is debased. Just ritually repeating these phrases is really aggression masked as assertion, because you would not really be taking the other person's views or feelings into account.

Sometimes, 'putting yourself in the other person's position' could lead you to behave nonassertively. So, for instance, if you see that a colleague is busy, you might say to yourself, 'Oh it wouldn't be fair to ask Sarah to help out', and as a result would not even ask her. In this case you are denying your right to ask and her right to say 'No'; you are taking a decision for the other person. Your empathy is spilling over into sympathy.

DISCREPANCY ASSERTION

By this we mean pointing out the discrepancy between what has previously been agreed and what is actually happening or about to happen. It often concludes with a statement of your needs and wants. So for instance:

- 'As I understood it, we agreed that project A was top priority. Now you're asking me to give more time to project B. I'd like to clarify which is now the priority'
- 'Mike, I remember in my recent appraisal you said you would delegate more of the correspondence work to me. I'm still keen to do that'

When to use discrepancy assertion

It is useful to regard discrepancy assertion as a *starting point* for when you suspect that there is a contradiction in what has been agreed and what is happening, or about to happen. It helps you to establish whether there is an actual contradiction, or whether there was simply a misunderstanding of the agreement between you and the other person. If there is a misunderstanding you can then clarify the issue and make a new agreement. If, on the other hand, there is a contradiction, you can go on and discover the reason for this, before taking further action. Thus, if the other person had merely forgotten the original agreement then your discrepancy assertion is usually sufficient to restore the status quo. On the other hand, if the person has chosen to ignore the previous agreement, then your discrepancy assertion makes it clear that you recall the agreement and wish it to stand. At the same time, it gives them the opportunity to revert back to the original agreement.

Or it brings out in the open the fact that they no longer feel bound by it. From here you can find out whether circumstances have changed to make the previous agreement impractical. If not, then you could use a basic assertion to restate that you would like the agreement to stand.

Discrepancy assertion can also be used when there is contradiction between a person's *present* words and deeds. For example, a colleague who says, 'I really think we could improve cooperation between your department and ours' and then launches into a lengthy attack on your staff: 'The trouble with your department is you've got too many people who think they know it all. They'll never ...; They don't ...; I can't ever see ... (etc.).' A discrepancy assertion will point out how this inconsistent behaviour is working against what they want. 'Hang on, Paul, on the one hand you are wanting to improve cooperation between our departments, but on the other hand you are making statements that make it difficult for us to cooperate. I agree with you that we *can* improve cooperation, so let's concentrate on that.' This also encourages the person to decide what they really want.

NEGATIVE FEELINGS ASSERTION
Here you are making a statement that draws the attention of another person to the undesirable effect their behaviour is having on you. So it can contain the following four elements, not necessarily in the order given:

1. When ...   (an objective description of other's behaviour).
2. The effects are ... (how that behaviour specifically affects you).
3. I feel ...   (a description of your feelings).
4. I'd like ...   (a statement of what you want or prefer).

An example is:
'*When* you let me have your return at this late stage,
it involves my working over the weekend.
I feel annoyed about this,
so in future *I'd like* to have it by Friday lunchtime.'

When to use negative feelings assertion
You can use this when the other person is still ignoring your rights in spite of your having raised an issue several times on previous occasions. Or you can use it when the person is repeatedly violating your rights during a single interaction. At this point you would be likely to experience very strong negative feelings—anger, resentment, hurt, and the like—and the advantage of negative feelings assertion is that it gives you a mechanism for expressing these feelings openly, without making an uncontrolled emotional outburst, and without denying these feelings exist. (For more guidance on handling negative feelings, see also Chapter 6.) So negative feelings assertion enables

you to take responsibility for your feelings and to express them assertively. In a later section we look at *how* to use this behaviour.

In addition, negative feelings assertion is very powerful in alerting the other person to the effects of their action on you—even without the 'I feel ...' part. You may not wish to talk of your feelings in some situations (for instance, with certain people or within certain organizational climates). In this case we suggest you omit the 'I feel' part, emphasize instead the 'when' and 'the effects' parts—without actually *blaming* the other person—and then state what you would like. In many cases this will be sufficient for the other person to agree to changes. In other cases the negative feelings assertion may be only a first step because it uncovers an underlying problem between you. Thus, in this example it may be that the late return resulted from an unrealistic workload. This then becomes the problem you need to resolve.

CONSEQUENCE ASSERTION

This informs the other person of the future consequences for them of *not* changing their behaviour. It also includes an opportunity to change that behaviour before the consequences occur. So, for instance:

- 'If you continue to withhold the information, I'm left with no option but to bring in the production director. I'd prefer not to'
- 'I'm not prepared, Jenny, to let any of my staff cooperate with yours on the project, unless you give them access to the same facilities that your people have'
- 'If this occurs again I'm left with no alternative but to apply the formal disciplinary procedure. I'd prefer not to'

When to use consequence assertion

As it is the strongest form of assertion, we see consequence assertion as a last-resort behaviour, to be used sparingly and only when the other types have failed. It is easy for consequence behaviour to be seen as threatening and thus aggressive. Some hints on how to reduce the chances of this happening are given later in this chapter.

You can use consequence assertion only when you have sanctions to apply. These might be: referring an issue to a higher level of management, giving a request a lower level of priority than usual, reducing a budget, limiting your cooperation, or applying a recognized disciplinary procedure. In addition, you can use consequence assertion only when you are *prepared* to apply the sanctions. Otherwise you would lose credibility. Even when you have sanctions and are prepared to use them, there is the question: 'What sanctions does the other person have to use in return?'

In the light of all this you might decide not to use a consequence assertion.

Then, the alternative is a negative feelings assertion, which emphasizes the 'I feel' part of the behaviour.

RESPONSIVE ASSERTION
We have listed this one last, not because it is least important, but because it is a rather different animal. The emphasis with this behaviour is upon *finding out where other people stand*—their needs, wants, opinions, feelings. This is often achieved by asking questions, but can also be done by statements making it clear that you would like to hear from them. Examples of both forms are:

- 'What are your reservations about the new approach?'
- 'How long can you give me to try and persuade her?'
- 'What problems does that create for you?'
- 'What would you prefer to do?'
- 'John, I'd like to hear your views on this one'
- 'I'd like you to say which approach is better from your department's point of view'

When to use responsive assertion
Responsive assertion is the *vehicle* for checking out that, in standing up for your own rights, you are not violating the rights of others. You would use it when the other person has behaved nonassertively—not speaking up at all, or doing so only indirectly—to find out what their needs, wants, opinions, etc. are. You would also use it, regardless of whether people have behaved aggressively, nonassertively, or assertively, when you want to know whether a particular course of action is acceptable to them. In addition, you would use responsive assertion when you want to collect information from people; for instance, 'Dave, what is the deadline for that project?' You would use it when you suspect there is a misunderstanding between you that could create difficulties. So you would check out your understanding of what the other person is saying, or find out their understanding of something.

So responsive assertion can be used on its own like this, or it can be used in conjunction with other types of assertion, especially basic, empathetic, and discrepancy. So statements like 'I'd like to take the overtime item first; how does that fit in with you?' not only make your preference clear, but also encourage the other person to say if this approach meets their needs. The responsive part of the statement has two effects. First, it increases the chances that your behaviour will be seen as assertive rather than aggressive. Following on from this, it increases the likelihood of the other person's responding assertively to this perceived assertion. This is particularly so when dealing with people who tend towards nonassertion. Responsive assertion, therefore, paves the way for interactions to become assertive/

assertive exchanges. This is crucial to assertiveness if both parties' needs are to be met and conflicts resolved (see Chapter 11).

We have described six types of assertion, together with examples of each. This information is summarized for easy reference in Table 5.1 at the end of the chapter. We have so far said specifically when you might use each of the different types. In the next section we make some general notes on using all these types of assertion.

When to use different assertions—general notes

As a guiding principle for deciding what type of assertiveness to use, we say: *use the minimum degree of assertion for achieving your aim*. For most situations this usually involves starting with lower levels and moving up to higher levels. So does this mean the types can be arranged into a strict hierarchy according to their strength? Not really, though you would probably agree with us that consequence is stronger than empathetic assertion. That apart, for convenience we usually divide the assertions into two levels:

- Lower level: basic, responsive, empathetic
- Higher level: discrepancy, negative feelings, consequence

Even so, this is a rough and ready distinction because the perceived strength of the behaviour will depend, among other things, on the words used and on the nonverbal behaviour. However, let us demonstrate the 'minimum degree' principle with the example of Jenny taking an item back to a shop. Her aim was to get the faulty item replaced with a good one.

JENNY: 'I bought this alarm clock here yesterday. The button for moving the hands isn't working properly so I'd like to exchange it.' *(Basic)*

The assistant could have agreed to exchange the clock, or he could have 'hassled' by saying something like:

ASSISTANT: 'We sell a lot of these but this is the first time we've had a complaint.'

Then Jenny could have replied:

JENNY: 'I appreciate that. However, I would still like it replaced.' *(Empathetic)*
or   *or*
'I would still like it replaced.' *(Basic)*

At this point the assistant may agree but may not. So after several exchanges Jenny would raise the level of assertion:

64

JENNY: 'I would like the item changed. If you are not   (*Consequence*)
prepared to do that I would like to talk to the
manager. I'd prefer it if we sorted it out.'

You might be wondering: 'Why not wade in straightaway with a consequence assertion—it would save a lot of time.' Unfortunately, we cannot prove or disprove this particular claim. But one of the snags with using a consequence or any of the higher levels of assertion too early in a situation is that you leave yourself with fewer options and thus less room for manoeuvre. After all, once you have stated a consequence, if the other person still ignores your rights then you either climb down or carry out the sanction! The danger is that you get locked into applying the sanctions against your better judgement.

Another snag with the 'shoot first, ask later' theory is that you never know whether your victim was innocent! So in the example of the shop assistant you would never know whether they *might* have agreed in response to a lower-level assertion. We are amazed how many of the tricky situations that *we* face can be resolved successfully with lower levels of assertion. But this is something for you to test out! Besides, you have nothing to lose—you can more easily move up the scale than down.

Undoubtedly, if you use a strong assertion early in a situation the other person will more likely perceive this as aggression. When this happens (unless they have learned to handle you assertively!) they respond with either aggression or nonassertion; whereas the aim in using the types of assertion is to get assertive—assertive exchanges, because the outcomes of these exchanges on the whole are more satisfactory to both parties.

Now that you are more familiar with the different types of assertion, you may have a concern about whether you would be seen as assertive in using some of them (for example, consequence or discrepancy). It will help enormously if you follow the 'minimum degree' principle. However, it is also crucial that your nonverbal behaviours and the actual words you use are clearly assertive. The next section aims to help you in these two areas.

How to say the types of assertion—assertively

It is quite possible to be seen as nonassertive or aggressive when using the six behaviours described above. It may be the actual words you use, or the nonverbal behaviours that accompany them. The rest of this section is intended to complement and take further the verbal and nonverbal characteristics of ass, agg, and na described in Chapter 2. We will look at the six types in turn.

65

BASIC ASSERTION

The only new point we wish to make here concerns repeating a basic assertion in order to re-emphasize your needs and wants. For your assertion to be seen as *stronger*, you can make it shorter than your initial statement, saying each word slower and louder than before, and giving more or less equal weight to each word: 'I . would . like . it . replaced.' Or you can make the repeat statements the same length as before, but giving more emphasis to the key words: 'I would *still* like to have it *replaced* with a *new* one.'

EMPATHETIC ASSERTION

We mentioned earlier that the important thing here is to avoid 'ritual' use of this behaviour. You can achieve this by slowing down and giving emphasis to the 'I understand/appreciate' part of the behaviour. The tone of voice needs to be warm and sincere rather than having a hint of exasperation or irritation in it. Good eye contact also helps to convey sincerity.

DISCREPANCY ASSERTION

When using this behaviour it is important to describe the discrepancy in a 'matter of fact' way; otherwise it comes across as accusing the other person of breaking an agreement. ('You *said* you were going to get that done by the end of last week': the spoken or unspoken message it ' . . . and it's your fault it hasn't been done.' This may be a risky assumption.) Making your statement in a matter of fact way means keeping your voice at a constant pace and not letting the pitch rise up at the end. Prefacing your statement with phrases that emphasize *your* interpretation of the agreement ('as I understood it'; 'the way I remember it') help to uncover misunderstandings at an early stage in the interaction.

NEGATIVE FEELINGS ASSERTION

These statements also can easily be seen as accusing and blaming. Saying them in a matter of fact way is again important. In addition, there are two other things you can do. One is to make your statement in the form of: 'When you do X, it leads to Y; I feel Z'—as opposed to: 'When you do X, it leads to Y; you make me feel Z'. This may seem a small distinction, but there is a dramatic difference in the meaning and effect of these two. In the second you are blaming the other person for making you feel the way you do—which is likely to bring forth an aggressive 'That's your problem' type reply, or a nonassertive apology. In the first version *you* are retaining responsibility for how you feel—which is more likely to lead to an assertive response: 'I wasn't aware of that' or 'that isn't what I intended'. We discuss the issue of responsibility for feelings in Chapter 6.

Second, be specific when you describe both the other person's behaviour and the concrete effects. So for example:

- 'When you continually disagree with other people's suggestions in our department meetings, it makes it difficult for us to reach agreement'

as opposed to:

- 'When you behave so negatively in our department meeting it really does make life difficult for me'

The more generalized the description of that person's behaviour, the more difficult it is for them to see the link between their behaviour and its effects. In turn, the more likely they are to take it as a personal attack and thus respond aggressively.

CONSEQUENCE ASSERTION

This type of assertion presents particular difficulties for many people because it is the strongest form of assertion. It is closest to aggression and so it can easily be seen as a threat. To avoid this, keep the words themselves factual, rather than emotional and personal. For example, 'If you do X, I will have no option but to do Y' is not a *personal* attack upon the other person, but a factual statement of what will happen. Again, describe 'X' and 'Y' in specific rather than generalized terms, avoiding statements like 'If you keep undermining my position, I'll have to retaliate'. Even where the words you use are assertive, you can be seen as threatening because of the accompanying nonverbal elements. Try saying the following consequence assertion out loud in different ways:

'If you continue to withhold the information, I'm left with no option but to bring in the production director. I'd prefer not to.'

Did you:

- Say it very quickly, voice rising towards 'the production director' bit?
- Drive home your meaning, say, by pointing your finger on the 'if you' part?
- Glare or slant your eyes at some imaginary person?
- Move your head or your body forward?

Then you would be likely to be seen as threatening or menacing. So, to give the information in a neutral way:

- Hold your voice at medium volume with steady pace and pitch
- Emphasize key words like verbs and nouns ('withhold', 'information', 'option', etc.) rather than pronouns ('you', 'me')
- Slow down the last sentence
- Keep your eye contact firm but not glaring and your head upright

We find also that phrases like 'I'd prefer not to', or 'I'd like to resolve this between ourselves' give the other person an opportunity to consider the consequences you have mentioned and decide whether, in the light of them, they wish to modify their behaviour in any way.

RESPONSIVE ASSERTION

Although a very different behaviour from consequence assertion, this can also be seen as threatening, as though the other person is being interrogated. The following question is intended to collect 'neutral' information:
'Peter, how long did you say it will take you to finish that report?'
Try saying it in various ways. It is possible to make it sound incredulous, or as if you are accusing him of lying, or as though you do not trust his judgement—all by different emphases, and inflections in the voice.

To avoid this we have found it useful to practise saying to yourself easy, 'seeking information'-type questions followed by more difficult questions— *both in the same tone of voice*. For instance 'Peter, what's the mileage to Manchester?' followed by 'Peter, what happened on your visit last week?'

Summary

By way of summary for this chapter, Table 5.1 pulls together into a convenient format the different types of assertion, with definition and examples of each.

In order to test your own understanding of the different types, we suggest you work through the recognition exercise in Table 5.2. You will probably find Table 5.1 a useful prompt for working through the exercise.

Table 5.1 Summary of types of assertion

Type	Definition	Examples
Basic	A straightforward statement that stands up for your rights by making clear your needs, wants, beliefs, opinions or feelings	'As I see it the system is working well.' 'I need to be away by 17.00 hours.' 'I feel very pleased with the way the issue has been resolved.'
Empathetic	A behaviour that contains an element of empathy as well as a statement of your needs and wants	'I appreciate that you don't like the new procedure, Jenny. However, until it's changed I'd like you to keep your people working to it.' 'I know you're busy at the moment, John. However, I'd like to make a quick request of you.'
Discrepancy	A statement that points out the difference between what has previously been agreed, and what is actually happening or about to happen	'Mike, in my recent appraisal I remember you saying that you would delegate more of the correspondence work to me. I'm still keen to do that.'
Negative feelings	A statement that draws the attention of another person to the undesirable effect that their behaviour is having on you. It can contain the following elements: • When … • The effects are … • I feel … • I'd like …	'*When* you let me have your return at this late stage, it involves me working over the weekend. *I feel* annoyed about this, *I'd like* in future to have it by Friday lunchtime.'
Consequence	A statement that informs the other person of the consequences for them of *not* changing their behaviour. It also gives them an opportunity to change that behaviour	'I'm not prepared, Jenny, to let any of my staff cooperate with yours on the project unless you give them access to the same facilities that your people have.' 'If this occurs again, I'm left with no alternative but to apply the formal disciplinary procedure. I'd prefer not to.'
Responsive	A behaviour that aims to find out where the other person stands, their needs, wants, opinions, and feelings	'What problems does that create for you?' 'What would you prefer to do?' 'John, I'd like to hear your views on this one.'

69

Table 5.2 Recognition exercise: Types of assertion

The following exercise contains 25 examples of assertive behaviours. You are asked to state what type of assertion each example is. The exercise is not intended as a test of memory, so please use Table 5.1 as an aid.

On each page there is space for you to write your answer in the *right*-hand column. Our suggested answer for each behaviour is given on the *line below* in the *left*-hand column. This will enable you to check your own answer before moving on to the next example.

Start by covering up all the answers on the left-hand side, and then reveal them, one at a time, to check your answers against ours.

At the end of the exercise, we suggest you look back to any examples where your answer differed from ours, and see if there is a particular type of assertion that is causing difficulty. If there is, we suggest you refer back to the text for the original definition and examples.

If you agree with 20 or more of the suggested answers, that is fine at this stage.

Suggested answer	Example	Your answer
↓	1. 'What ideas do you have for improving the existing methods?'	
Responsive	2. 'There are about 15 people involved.'	
Basic	3. 'At this stage I'm not sure I want to get involved. I'd like time to think about it.'	
Basic	4. 'Mike, when you continually interrupt me while I'm working on the balance sheets, it means I have to start all over again. I'm feeling irritated by this, so I'd prefer you to wait till I finish a sheet.'	
Negative feelings	5. 'I thought we said we'd limit the scope of the research, but now you're talking of further developments. I'd rather stick with our plan, and keep the developments 'til later.'	
Discrepancy	6. 'How do you think that will work out? Will there be any problems?'	
Responsive	7. 'I'd like you to take this request seriously; otherwise we'll discuss it with the department head. I'd prefer not to.'	
Consequence	8. 'Dave, I recognize that you're wanting to chat for a while. However, I don't want to spend any more time now. I'd like to get on with this report.'	

Table 5.2 *(continued)*

Suggested answer	*Example*	*Your answer*
Empathetic	9. 'I'm pleased with the work we've produced. I think it will lead to a lot of developments.'	
Basic	10. 'It hasn't worked that way in my experience.'	
Basic	11. 'Mike, I'd like you to say whether you agree or not.'	
Responsive	12. 'As I remember it, you agreed to send the paperwork with the order because it helps our system. Recently, the two have been arriving separately. I would prefer it if they came together.'	
Discrepancy	13. 'Jim, when will you have the order ready?'	
Responsive	14. 'What I meant by that is we may not always have the time.'	
Basic	15. Sue, I realize that you are wanting to move on to the next stage. However, I'd like you to stick with this 'til we get agreement.'	
Empathetic	16. 'I suggest we incorporate that into the last section.'	
Basic	17. 'John, when you say things like that, it sounds like you're taking the department for granted. I don't feel happy about that. So in future, I'd like you to check with one of us before committing us to extra work.'	
Negative feelings	18. 'Jackie, in future, unless you consult me beforehand, I won't be prepared to commit myself to meet your new deadlines. Now I don't want it to get to that stage.'	
Consequence	19. 'When you say "the operation", which people are you including in that?'	

Table 5.2 *(continued)*

Suggested answer	Example	Your answer
Responsive	20. 'Shall we work on the list separately and then check our results at the end?'	
Responsive	21. 'I know you haven't liked working with Pete. However, I believe the two of you would be the best ones to sort out the "new design" problems.'	
Empathetic	22. 'On the whole, I go along with that idea as long as we can iron out a few problems with it.'	
Basic	23. 'On the one hand you have agreed to improve the arrangements for our department, but now you are dismissing the problems we raise. I'd like to get it clear what the position is.'	
Discrepancy	24. 'Margaret, why do you think it will cause problems?'	
Responsive	25. 'Chris, you're still taking a long time with the first part, which means I have to rush the second part to get it all out on time. I'm feeling irritated by this, so I'd like you to suggest what we can do to speed up the first part.'	
Negative feelings		

6. Handling negative feelings

People often say to us they have succeeded in making changes in their *behaviour*—so for much of the time they can behave assertively—but there are still times when they have such strong negative *feelings* that they have difficulty in being assertive. This may have happened to you also. For instance, have you experienced any of the following:

- Feeling angry about a sarcastic remark from someone and responding with an aggressive retort which leads to a prolonged row?
- Feeling worried about your manager's reaction and being unable to ask her for a regrading of your job?
- Feeling very frustrated about the service you are getting from a colleague and blowing your top when you next see him?
- Feeling guilty about imposing on a colleague and not asking her for assistance even though you are rushed off your feet?

The above statements, while not necessarily reflecting your feelings accurately, may have prompted you to think of similar incidents and the accompanying feelings. What is important to note is that because of your feelings you then behaved in certain ways.

Some of the feelings you experience—excitement, enthusiasm, confidence, concern—we would call *productive* feelings. They are useful in leading you to behave effectively: preparing systematically, speaking clearly, stating facts as you see them, replying calmly. Some of the feelings—extreme anger, worry, frustration, guilt, jealousy, depression, inadequacy—are much more negative, and we call them *unproductive* feelings. They make it difficult for you to behave effectively and in ways that you would like. So you mumble your words, 'blow your top', back off issues that are important to you, 'run round in circles' when preparing.

Essentially, this book is about developing assertive *behaviour*. But we recognize that, if we deal exclusively with behaviour, then the process of changing would not always be successful. The behaviour changes would be hindered by the strong feelings you would still be experiencing. So this chapter steps back from the behaviour to work on the feelings that affect behaviour. It looks at the way many people handle feelings, where the feelings come from, the nature of thinking processes, and a strategy for handling unproductive feelings.

The way many people handle feelings

Many people believe that feelings are instinctive, part of the total package they start out with at birth. Because of this they think they are 'stuck' with various feelings. You often hear people saying things like 'He easily feels hurt. He can't help it. He's over-sensitive'; or 'She's always feeling angry about something or other. That's Jean for you'. If you believe that feelings are the result of your genetic make up, like the colour of your eyes, then you have only two options when it comes to handling them.

OPTION 1. STIFLE YOUR FEELINGS

By this, people usually mean don't give any outward expression to your emotions. This is also encouraged by various socialization messages like 'We're British, we don't show our emotions'; or 'It's not ladylike to stamp your feet'; and 'Men don't cry'. This idea of suppressing your feelings probably originated at the same time as the Victorian corset—the effects are pretty similar, too! The trouble with stifling your feelings is that they don't actually go away. You merely experience them internally, while externally you exhibit behaviour that is out of line with your feelings. This gap between the behaviour and the feelings creates enormous stress which tends to show itself in headaches, nervous tension, and the like.

OPTION 2. GIVE VENT TO YOUR FEELINGS

This implies expressing your feelings freely in outward behaviour, regardless of when, where, and with whom. Certainly, if you exercise this option you may not suffer the side effects that go with stifling your feelings; but you may well create other problems for yourself, particularly in the reactions you get from other people. It would be a pretty daunting prospect if everyone openly expressed all of their feelings all the time!

Both of these options leave much to be desired, and many people who go for one rather than the other do so because it seems the lesser of two evils. This is the dilemma if you believe feelings are *instinctive*. In the next section we question this belief. This then opens up the possibility of a *third* option for handling unproductive feelings—without the stress of stifling them inwards; without the undesirable repercussions of giving vent to them.

Where feelings come from

SOME FEELINGS ARE INSTINCTIVE

There is controversy among physiologists and psychologists as to what constitutes feelings and where they come from. There is agreement that most of the physiological sensations we experience—heart pounding, shallow breathing, dry mouth—are instinctive, in that they are with us from birth. They are not usually under our conscious control but are automatically triggered in certain situations. For instance, when we hear a strange, loud, and unexpected noise there are automatic increases in our heart rate, blood pressure, and rate of breathing. All these prepare the body to act for our survival by 'fighting' or 'fleeing'.

SOME FEELINGS ARE LEARNED

Feelings such as anger, hurt, and worry may be accompanied by various of our inborn physiological sensations. It is likely also that these feelings have been developed during a lengthy process of learning from experience. It is difficult to say categorically which feelings are inborn and which are learned, but there is general agreement that we were not born feeling jealous, guilty, or nervous. So how do these feelings arise? Let us answer this question first with two examples, and then with a diagram of what is happening in the examples.

Example 1

Situation	You are on your way to speak to a client who has complained about one of the machines your firm installed recently. He has previously taken up a lot of your time with similar complaints.
Your thinking process	'It's typical of people like him. He's a nuisance. He just likes complaining. He's no right to take up my time like this. I won't let him rabbit on at length.'
Your feelings	Frustration, anger, impatience
Your behaviour	You don't really listen to his complaints to see if they are valid. You interrupt him and give the impression that you need to be away. (*aggression*)

Example 2

Situation	You are about to give a presentation to a group of senior managers. You have only done one presentation before.
Your thinking process	'Presentations are pretty demanding. All these managers will know more than me. They'll try and catch me out. I'll never be able to answer their questions. That will be awful.'
Your feelings	Worry, strong anxiety, panic, helplessness
Your behaviour	Stumbling over your words, hesitating or speaking too quickly, changing your mind too easily when questioned. (*nonassertion*)

The diagram in Figure 6.1 represents what is happening in these and similar situations.

75

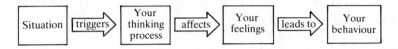

Figure 6.1   Relationship of thoughts, feelings and behaviour

THE IMPLICATIONS OF THIS MODEL

The total process, of course, is more complex than this, in that there are loopbacks from your feelings to your thinking process, which in turn have a spiralling effect on your feelings. However, what this model implies is that:

- Your feelings do *not* arise 'out of the blue'; they come about as a *result* of an external situation and your thinking process
- Your feelings are *not* controlled by events or other people; they are controlled by you and your thinking processes

If this was not so, then you would be at the entire mercy of events and other people. You would be blaming them for how you felt; they would be in control of you—a pretty dreary prospect.

But the examples and the model suggest that it is your *thinking process* about the situation that affects the type and strength of the feelings you have—for instance, whether you feel deep anxiety or only concern. The exciting thing about this proposition is that it opens up the opportunity for you to *gain more control* of your feelings—not to stifle them or to give them a free rein, but to modify or change them in any way you want, and even to express them openly and honetly in an *assertive* way (for example, using 'negative feelings assertion' described in Chapter 5). Just as you can bring your *behaviour* into your conscious control, so you can bring your *feelings* into your control and make them your responsibility.

You may be saying to yourself, if people *do* have this choice over their feelings, how come they choose to have *unproductive* feelings?

WHY PEOPLE HAVE UNPRODUCTIVE FEELINGS

As we have already said, many feelings—both productive and unproductive—occur as a result of thinking processes, which in turn are triggered by external situations. In addition, people frequently experience payoffs for certain of their feelings, that is to say, 'rewards' that follow *after* the feelings. When this happens people repeat those feelings and drop the ones that do not lead to satisfactory payoffs. So over a period of time these rewarded feelings become *learned*—part of the 'feelings repertoire'—even though they may be a hindrance to effective behaviour. The payoffs are sometimes difficult to identify, but we know, for instance, that, strange as it may seem, people can actually *enjoy* feeling helpless, inadequate, rejected, miserable, angry. Maybe the physiological sensations that accompany the feelings are pleasant to experience, or maybe they become familiar. There is also some comfort in the *self-fulfilling* effects of people's behaviour on their beliefs about themselves. Let us give an example of what we mean. If you believe you are a worrier, you will seek to experience worry because this confirms your picture of yourself both in your eyes and other people's.

In addition to wallowing in unproductive feelings, people often find that these feelings lead to behaviours that themselves have short-term payoffs. We have already mentioned this in Chapter 1, so here is just a brief example. Feeling hurt could lead you to say things that frequently succeed in getting people to feel sorry for you, and then to give way to you.

BY WAY OF SUMMARY

So far we have said:

- Some feelings are productive, in that they lead to effective behaviour
- Some feelings are unproductive, leading to ineffective behaviour
- Some feelings, like physiological sensations such as heart pounding, are inborn and are not usually under conscious control
- Some feelings, like jealousy, guilt, and worry, are learned as a result of experiences and the possible payoffs that accompany them
- These feelings follow after external situations and thinking processes, rather than being caused by situations or other people
- These feelings can be brought under conscious control

Of course, feelings that occur out of force of habit become so deeply rooted that you may not realize you can actually make choices about them. The thinking process that leads to these feelings occurs so rapidly that you may not always be aware it exists. In the next section we look more closely at the nature of this thinking process, and in the last section we show how to intervene in the thinking process in order to gain more control over feelings.

Meanwhile you might find it useful to break off at this stage to try out this exercise:

- Think back to a time when, as a result of a particular situation, your feelings were very strong and you behaved less effectively than you would have liked – either aggressively or nonassertively.
- What was the *situation* that triggered it all off; what might you have been *thinking* about the situation; what were the *feelings* you experienced?

The nature of the thinking process

We use the phrase 'thinking process' to refer to all of the things you think about a situation. It can be triggered before a situation, during, or after it. Initially we will concentrate on the thinking process that takes place before a situation, because, as you will see in the next section, these are easier to bring under your conscious control to start with. So, your thinking process *before* a situation can consist of any or all of the following thoughts, not necessarily in this order:

- *Memory* of a similar past situation
- *Image* of the situation in question, of yourself and others in the situation
- *Rights* in the situation (for detail on rights, see Chapter 3)
- *Obligations* and how you should appear to others; their obligations to you or to others
- *Anticipation* of your/their behaviour in that situation
- Possible *consequences* for you of these behaviours

Let us give an example of the thinking process in action, together with the resultant feelings and behaviour. The situation we have chosen is a frequent one we experience as trainers and may be familiar to you in your work—giving a presentation to a group of managers. So let us assume you are giving a presentation next week.

Your possible thinking process

'That previous presentation was a disaster. There were lots of awkward questions that I struggled to answer.'

Memory of a similar past experience

↓

'The presentation will be very tough. It's testing my expertise. I'll be on show.'

Image of the situation and yourself within it

↓

'They have no right to try and catch me out. I have the right to get my own back if they do.'

Their rights/your rights in the situation

↓

'I must have all the correct answers. I have to look as though I know my stuff.'

Your obligations/the way you should appear

↓

'They'll all ask lots of difficult questions; they always do. They'll disagree with my answers.'

Anticipation of their behaviour

↓

'I'll get sucked into lots of arguments that I'll lose. That would undermine my position. I can't have that.

Consequences for you of their behaviour

↓

'I'll really show them up if they try   Anticipation of your behaviour
to catch me out.'

Your likely feelings
These could vary from anger and resentment to determination and even
stubborness.

Your probable behaviour
You would tend to select material   *Before the presentation*
that impresses rather than helps
understanding.
You would be likely to curtail any   *During the presentation*
discussion abruptly, and respond to
'innocent' questions with put-downs
like 'If you'd been listening earlier
. . .'.

(aggression)

SOUND THINKING PROCESSES
Some of the thoughts you have are *sound*, in that they are a rational, honest,
and reasonably accurate reflection of the situation. When this is so they
result in feelings—like enthusiasm, excitement, happiness, regret, annoyance, mild frustration, concern, sadness, confidence—that are productive.
They goad you into assertive behaviour—into taking appropriate action—
that gives you control over yourself and over the situation.

FAULTY THINKING PROCESSES
Some of the thoughts you have are *faulty*, like most of the ones in the above
example, in that they are an irrational, not always honest, and aften inaccu-
rate reflection of the situation. These faulty thinking processes result in
feelings—like extreme anger, resentment, jealousy, rage, deep frustration,
worry, pity, helplessness, despair, depression—that are unproductive. They
lead you into nonassertive or aggressive behaviour—either into taking no
action or inappropriate action—that takes the control away from yourself.

WHAT MAKES SOME THINKING PROCESSES FAULTY?
We ask you to look at Table 6.1 for some answers to this question. There we
have taken the *faulty* aspects of the thinking process from the above example
and set out the flaws in these, together with some challenges to them.
    To sum up, many thinking processes are faulty because:

● They deal in extremes and exaggerations such as 'all', 'everyone', 'disaster', 'catastrophe', 'awful', 'terrible'

Table 6.1   Challenges to faulty thinking processes

Faulty thinking process	Flaw	Challenge
That previous presentation was a disaster.	Exaggeration	Is this accurate? Or did only parts of it go badly?
The presentation will be tough.	Generalizing from one event	Is this inevitable just because the previous one was tough?
It's testing my expertise. I'll be on show.	Ignoring important aspects	This may be the most important aspect to you but not necessarily to others.
They have no right to try and catch me out. I have the right to get my own back if they do.	Denying all rights Confusing rights	But don't they have the right to ask questions? Even if people have denied your rights, does this give you the right to stand up for your rights aggressively?
I must have all the correct answers. I have to look as though I really know my stuff.	Unrealistic expectations that follow some hidden 'rule book'	Why? What is so terrible about • Being wrong sometimes? • Not having all the answers? • Not knowing something?
They'll ask lots of difficult questions. They always do.	Assumptions generalizing	Are the 'all' and 'lots' guaranteed, or might it be 'some'? Will all the questions necessarily be difficult?
They'll disagree with my answers.	Illogical conclusion	Is this bound to be so?
I'll get sucked into lots of arguments that I will lose.	Exaggeration and assumption	'Lots' or only some arguments? Will you necessarily lose them?
That would undermine my position and I can't have that.	Illogical	Is this probable, or merely possible? Totally or only slightly?
I'll really show them up if they try to catch me out.	Relinquishing control of yourself	Or could you respond assertively if you chose to?

Table 6.2   Intervention strategy before a situation

Steps	Notes
1. Identify a situation	Concentrate on a situation: • That you initiate yourself or know of in advance • That is likely to happen in the next week • That you know will give rise to strong feelings and thus will make it difficult for you to behave assertively (you may know this from similar situations in the past) (A likely situation could be: a meeting, your appraisal, appraising your staff, raising a difficult issue with your manager, a colleague or a customer.)
2. Start the intervention	After identifying a situation you may already be started on your thinking process, or experiencing strong unproductive feelings, so *intervene with your inner dialogue*. Ask yourself 'what am I saying to myself?' Do not veto your faulty thinking at this stage—it is a good idea to get your *worst* thinking out into your dialogue. So your dialogue may be a mixture of faulty and sound elements. Make sure it contains at least: your anticipated behaviour; their anticipated behaviour; and the consequences of these for you. These should include the worst that could happen (Table 6.3 gives examples of what we mean).
3. Challenge faulty inner dialogue	Challenge all the faulty elements by looking out for exaggerations, assumptions, and the like (see Tables 6.1 and 6.3 for examples of challenges).
4. Convert faulty dialogue into sound dialogue	Retain any sound elements. Replace all the faulty elements with corresponding sound ones. Be certain that your sound dialogue includes at least: your rights; their rights in the situation; and your anticipated behaviour. The aim is not to give yourself a 'pep' talk with statements of the impossible, but to be realistic and rational (Table 6.3 has examples of sound dialogue).
5. Talk through the sound dialogue	Talk through the sound inner dialogue to yourself until you are comfortable and familiar with it (out loud is even better).
6. Describe your feelings	Try and describe what you now feel about the situation. Your feelings should be of the *productive* variety, e.g. concern, confidence, irritation, excitement, enthusiasm, annoyance, sadness, happiness, etc. If not, then you may still have a lurking faulty inner dialogue that needs challenging more strongly. Or you may need to repeat your sound dialogue to yourself once more. The aim is to *modify* any strong unproductive feelings, *not* to change them dramatically. For instance, it is better to modify deep anxiety into concern rather than try to feel carefree!

- They reach conclusions about the 'inevitability' of things
- They make generalizations from scant evidence of one event, or one or two people, with labels like: 'typical'; 'they're all the same'
- They ignore some aspects of the situation
- They deal in absolutes of right/wrong, black/white, good/bad
- They place unrealistic expectations on people and on events such as: 'I must'; 'I have to'; 'I ought'; 'They must'; 'They shouldn't; 'It's not fair'

In the next section we show how to deal with faulty thinking processes in order to gain control over unproductive feelings which push you into nonassertion or aggression (as in the example given).

Handling unproductive feelings

People can be successful in modifying and changing their feelings without stifling them or giving vent to them. They are various strategies for this, but the one we have personally found useful, and the one many managers find practical, is to *intervene* in the thinking process. As we have said earlier, the thinking process usually occurs so rapidly that you may not always be aware of it. So one way to slow it down is to intervene with what we will call an *inner dialogue*, that is, talking your thinking process over to yourself.

INTERVENING WITH AN INNER DIALOGUE BEFORE A SITUATION
The diagram in Figure 6.2 shows how the intervention works. We are going to concentrate on using inner dialogue before a situation. This will enable you to control your feelings prior to the situation so that your behaviour both before and during the situation will more likely be assertive. The intervention is easiest to practise at this stage because you get more time to slow down the thinking process. Table 6.2 gives more detail on the steps of the intervention already outlined in Figure 6.2. We invite you to try it out.

Table 6.3 gives examples of working through the intervention strategy in two different situations. These examples are derived from our own and other people's experiences of using the intervention strategy. So they may not ring true for you—your own examples will be more real. Your examples may not contain as much detail as ours. This does not matter, because we were merely covering many possibilities for demonstration purposes. What is important is for you to include in your sound dialogue statements about your antici-pated behaviour of the '*I can*' variety. These need to be a realistic reflection of your capabilities, so that they push you into planning your behaviour—exactly what you will say and do. You can then rehearse your assertive behaviour to yourself.

As you become accustomed to using the intervention strategy of inner dialogues you will find that you will make less use of Step 3—'challenge';

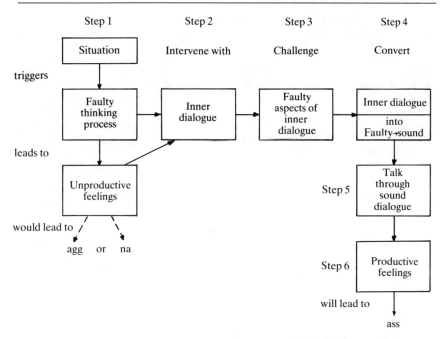

Figure 6.2 Intervening with an inner dialogue

instead, you automatically convert faulty dialogue into sound. Gradually you get to the point where inner dialogues consist of fewer faulty thoughts anyway. Using an inner dialogue intervention *before* a situation soon has a spin off effect on you *during* a situation.

INTERVENING DURING A SITUATION

To be realistic, you would be unlikely to intervene in the thinking process *during* a situation until you were practised at doing it *before* a situation. Even then, the thinking process happens so quickly during most interactions that you would not have time to work through all the steps of the intervention in Table 6.2. Nevertheless, it is possible to intervene especially during situations where you went through the full intervention strategy beforehand. Table 6.4 sets out this shorter intervention. There are examples in Table 6.5 of sound inner dialogues for using during an interaction.

INTERVENING AFTER A SITUATION

If someone bursts into your office giving you no chance to hold an inner dialogue with yourself before the situation and little time during, then it's a good idea to work through one afterwards. Already you might be accustomed to thinking things over as you drive home in the car ('if only I'd said

83

Table 6.3   Examples of intervention strategy before a situation

Situation	Possible faulty inner dialogue	Challenge	Sound inner dialogue
1. John, a member of staff, has again made mistakes in the invoices. You have told him before about this. You are about to see him.	There'll be a row this time.	Is this inevitable?	There'll probably be an uncomfortable exchange.
	He has no right to make a mess of these invoices.	Are you denying him his rights?	He has the right to make mistakes. He has the responsibility not to keep repeating them.
	I have the right to really tear him off a strip.	Violating his rights just because he seems to be violating yours?	I have the right to get him to improve and to accept his responsibility.
	He doesn't care. It's typical of his generation. He'll make some excuse just to 'fob me off'.	'Care' and 'typical' based on what evidence? Is an 'excuse' 100% certain to happen?	He may not care, but that need not hinder his work. There may be excuses, but they need not 'fob me off'. There may be reasons behind the excuses.
	That would totally undermine my position.	Are you really that vulnerable?	That might affect me a little.
	I can't have that. I'll show him. I'll get really mad.	Who is in control of you?	*I can* stand it if I choose to. *I can* point out the effects of his mistakes without getting mad.
	↓		↓
	unproductive feelings—rage vindictiveness		productive feelings— annoyance
	↓		↓
	aggressive behaviour —'Why can't you get this right? I've told you before ... '.		assertive behaviour —'... these mistakes are causing me problems ... Why are they occurring?

Table 6.3 *(continued)*

Situation	Possible faulty inner dialogue	Challenge	Sound inner dialogue
2. You have a report to finish by the end of the week. You are short of time.	This report will be circulated to a lot of people.		
	Some of them are senior to me. They'll know more about it than me.	Is this necessarily so?	Some of them might know more than me.
	This means they are more capable than me.	Does this follow?	Knowing more doesn't make them more capable.
	They'll pick holes in it. They'll pull it to bits.	All of them? Is this ignoring some aspects of the situation?	Some of them may criticize it; some may like it.
	That would be dreadful.	Would it?	It will be disappointing if some don't like it, but not dreadful.
	I've got to get every word right.	Is this realistic?	It would be nice to get it word perfect, but this isn't realistic.
	I mustn't leave anything out.	What if something were left out?	Some of the less important things could be left out.
	I'll never get it sorted out.	Never?	It may take time but *I can* sort it out.
	↓		↓
	unproductive feelings—hopelessness, panic		productive feelings—concern confidence
	↓		↓
	nonassertive behaviour—oscillating between frantic disorganized activity and of helplessness.		assertive behaviour—writing an *acceptable* first draft and improving it if time

Table 6.4   Intervention strategy during a situation

Steps	Notes
1. Take a deep breath	While the other person is talking or just before you respond.
2. Recall your sound dialogue	Talk through at least the part of it that deals with their behaviour and the 'I can' statements. Make them apply to the present instead of the future. (Table 6.5 gives examples of these.)
3. Slow down your response	Do this by starting your response with slow, firm words or phrases such as 'Well', 'I see', 'Let me see', 'Fine', 'Yes'. This buys you time to collect at least your first sentence together.

Table 6.5   Examples of sound inner dialogues during a situation

Situation	Sound inner dialogue
1. Steve, a colleague, is reluctant to agree to firm deadlines. He keeps stating difficulties.	I'm feeling frustrated but I can control it. I can tell Steve why. Then I'll begin to get somewhere. I can repeat my need for firm deadlines. I needn't get impatient.
2. Margaret, a member of staff, is very edgy when you refuse a request for time off.	She's getting upset. She may get angry. That needn't put me off balance. I have the right to refuse. I needn't be rude to her. I can continue to be assertive.

that'). If you find yourself replaying things over and over again and feeling more sick with each replay, then you have a faulty inner dialogue! In Table 6.6 we include some faulty and corresponding sound inner dialogues.

Inner dialogues after a situation enable you to learn from it. So it is important not to gloss over successes as if they were trivial. It is a myth that people learn only from failures. Successes enable you to know what might be worth repeating another time. Similarly, it is useful to analyse failures but not to berate yourself because of them. There are likely to be elements of success and failure in most situations, so why not work to increase the success and reduce the failure?

Table 6.6   Inner dialogues after a situation

Situation	Faulty inner dialogue	Sound inner dialogue
1. You put forward your idea to senior managers for a change in reporting levels. They rejected your idea.	It's awful that I can't get senior managers to see why they need to change. It's typical of the narrow view they take. I might as well give up.	If I can't get them to change it is frustrating, but not awful. It may be narrow in my eyes but that doesn't mean it *is* narrow. I can begin to make plans to minimize the effect on me.
2. You started to behave assertively to your colleague but lost it when the going got rough.	I might have known it wouldn't work with Tom. He deserved that—accusing me of lying. He really makes my blood boil.	It will be difficult with Tom but not impossible. Next time I can keep going longer. He may aggravate me, but I needn't rise to the bait. I can keep my cool—I'll take a deep breath next time.

Summary

In this chapter we have stepped back from observable behaviour and have considered:

- How feelings affect behaviour
- How thinking processes lead to feelings
- How to intervene in thinking processes with inner dialogues
- Challenges to faulty inner dialogues
- How to convert a faulty dialogue into a sound one

This enables you to modify unproductive feelings into productive ones and then to behave assertively.

In later chapters we continue to refer to inner dialogues.

7. Giving and receiving criticism about performance

Talking about unsatisfactory aspects of performance is one of the most difficult tasks that people at work have to face—whether they are giving or receiving criticism. It is made difficult because many people almost equate performance of the job with competence as a person. Clearly this is an illfounded conclusion and yet it is often the basis (either for the giver or for the receiver) of much of the criticism of performance that occurs at work. Think how often criticism about job performance turns into an attack upon the person themselves, think how often the person concerned perceives themselves under attack.

You yourself may have had unwelcome experiences either making or taking criticism. This chapter aims to help you avoid such experiences by introducing some guidelines in giving criticism *assertively*, either to staff or to a colleague. This is followed by some hints on how to behave assertively when *receiving* criticism.

Giving criticism

When faced with someone's unsatisfactory performance, have you found yourself:

- Avoiding raising the particular criticism, or raising it very tentatively? *(nonassertion)*
- Working yourself into an angry state so that you raise the issue in an abrupt heavy-handed way? *(aggression)*

In these cases, either the required change in the person's performance does not come about, or if it does it is accompanied by some undesirable changes. Maybe the person ends up saying 'OK, if that's what you want me to do in future, I'll do it.' At the same time they may be *saying to themselves*, 'But don't expect me to help out the next time you've got a rush on.' Neither of these is a satisfactory outcome, and likely as not the relationship between you gets worse.

Let us begin by stating that criticizing performance is not an end in itself; it is done to achieve a particular goal. The goal is *a change in the way a person carries out a particular aspect of their job*. It is easy to lose sight of this end and to become addicted to the means. Many people see criticizing itself as the all-important thing; as long as they do this they think they are 'managing'. Criticizing is seen as 'just a matter of a two-minute ticking off, then all will be well'. Sadly, all will most certainly *not* be well. This approach gives criticism a negative feel to it (one of the reasons we hesitated about even using the word in the first place). Let us stress that we see criticism as a *constructive* event—with emphasis on future changes for improvement rather than on the error of past ways, with follow-up afterwards, if necessary, to check progress.

So, armed with this positive rather than destructive image of giving criticism, we will now consider the rights of the people involved.

RIGHTS INVOLVED IN CRITICISM

If you want to use criticism as a legitimate means of helping a person improve their performance, then you are more likely to be effective if you make your criticism assertively. In order to do this you need to accept that you have the *right* to want people to improve their performance. Following on from this, you need to accept the right to criticize that performance. The *responsibility* that goes with this right is to criticize in a way that does not attack the person, put them down, or make them look small. Even though they have made mistakes, repeated mistakes, or failed to improve, they have *not* forfeited their right to be treated assertively. In other words, their mistakes do not give you the right to behave aggressively.

To behave assertively also requires you to have sound inner dialogues about the particular situation and the person you intend to criticize.

SOME COMMON INNER DIALOGUES

In Table 7.1 are some examples of common faulty dialogues concerning giving criticism, and some equivalent sound ones. Faulty dialogues 1–4 will result in your behaving aggressively; 5 and 6 will lead to nonassertion. The last one will result in nonassertion in the short run, but aggression when you do eventually raise the issue with Andy. The first faulty dialogue is an example of violating the rights of someone who has made a mistake.

Faulty dialogue 5 is an example of how the anticipation of the other person's nonassertion influences your behaviour. Faulty dialogue 6 indicates a similar thing with anticipation of aggression. More about this in Chapter 8.

GUIDELINES FOR GIVING CRITICISM

The guidelines we give in Figure 7.1 are intended for use when making those 'everyday' criticisms of performance, for example when someone produces a report that is not to the agreed standard. They can also be used in conjunction with the hints (earlier in the book) for giving praise, because there are usually good as well as bad aspects to a particular piece of work. It would be

Table 7.1 Inner dialogues about giving criticism

	Faulty inner dialogues	*Sound inner dialogues*
1.	I have the right to really tear John off a strip when I talk to him about the mess he made of his budget forecasts.	Just because John has made mistakes, he has not forfeited his right to be treated assertively. I can point out how his budget forecasts affected me.
2.	I've spoken to Sally twice before about this. She's just being awkward.	I've spoken to Sally twice before about this. I won't assume she is being awkward. She may have forgotten. I can remind her firmly without getting mad.
3.	If I give Mike half a chance, he'll start blaming me or others for his poor presentation yesterday. I'll make it clear from the beginning that I'm not going to stand for that.	Mike may start blaming me or others. If he does I can listen. Some of his points may be valid. I can get him to see why I think the presentation was poor.
4.	It was disastrous that Ann made that mistake.	Ann's mistake created real problems but was not disastrous. I can point them out. I can keep my cool. I can get her to change.
5.	If I raise this issue with Simon he's sure to get upset; that would be embarrassing. I would hate that.	Simon doesn't *always* get upset when I raise issues of this kind with him. If he does it may be embarrassing, but I can live with that.
6.	If I mention his mistakes to him, he's sure to fly off the handle. That would be terrible.	Even if he does fly off the handle, I believe I can cope with it.
7.	I won't make an issue of it this time, it'll look petty. But if Andy does it again, that will be it.	I'll raise it with Andy now, while it's still only a small irritation. He may think it's petty but it will stop a bigger blow up later on.

important to bring out both these aspects when you are dealing with some of the larger parts of a person's job—for instance, managing a project.

The approach we suggest will in most cases be used with the staff working for you, but it can also be used when you are unhappy about an aspect of a colleague's performance—for example, when they are sending their monthly return to you late.

Figure 7.1 summarizes the steps we suggest for giving criticism assertively and includes some examples. Following these steps increase the chances that you will reach agreement on any desired changes.

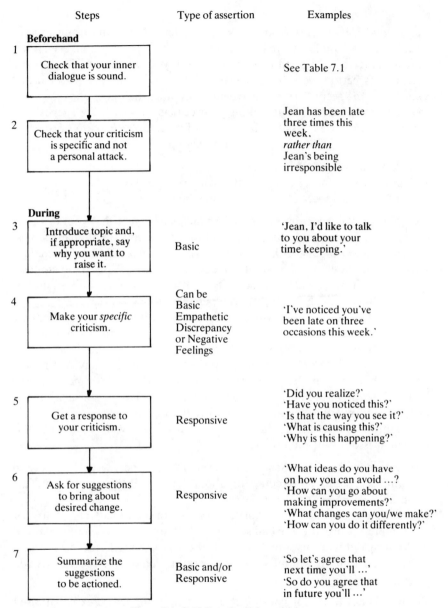

Steps	Type of assertion	Examples
Beforehand		
1 Check that your inner dialogue is sound.		See Table 7.1
2 Check that your criticism is specific and not a personal attack.		Jean has been late three times this week, *rather than* Jean's being irresponsible
During		
3 Introduce topic and, if appropriate, say why you want to raise it.	Basic	'Jean, I'd like to talk to you about your time keeping.'
4 Make your *specific* criticism.	Can be Basic Empathetic Discrepancy or Negative Feelings	'I've noticed you've been late on three occasions this week.'
5 Get a response to your criticism.	Responsive	'Did you realize?' 'Have you noticed this?' 'Is that the way you see it?' 'What is causing this?' 'Why is this happening?'
6 Ask for suggestions to bring about desired change.	Responsive	'What ideas do you have on how you can avoid ...?' 'How can you go about making improvements?' 'What changes can you/we make?' 'How can you do it differently?'
7 Summarize the suggestions to be actioned.	Basic and/or Responsive	'So let's agree that next time you'll ...' 'So do you agree that in future you'll ...'

Figure 7.1 Guidelines for giving criticism

Notes on the guidelines

Steps 1 and 2. Frequently you will be taking the initiative in raising an issue with someone. You therefore have time to do a little preparation, even if it is only a matter of two or three minutes before you go and see that person. During this period, you can check that your inner dialogue is sound and your criticism specific. As we have dealt with inner dialogues above, we will say a few more words about making your criticism specific. We suggest you describe as clearly as possible that aspect of a person's *observable behaviour* that you would like to see changed. For example:

- Taking too long over lunch breaks
- Not following the agreed format when writing a report
- Criticizing members of staff in the presence of others

Expressing criticisms in this factual form helps to ensure that your criticism is not seen as a personal attack. Generalized statements ('You made a mess of that') are too vague for the person to visualize what they have to change. Personalized statements ('Your attitude is all wrong' or 'You're too autocratic') are about traits such as personality or attitudes that not only cannot be observed but are likely to be seen as a personal attack.

Step 3. This is concerned with setting the scene by announcing the topic for discussion *before* getting immersed in the detail of the particular criticism you want to make. This eases the way into the criticism so that it is not seen as a 'bolt from the blue'. (Remember, the other person may have their mind on something else at the time.) It also helps you get to the point of the interaction, rather than beating about the bush. The latter approach smacks of nonassertion and often makes the other person suspicious.

It can also be useful at this step to say why you want to discuss this particular issue. You can do this by:

- Mentioning how the issue has arisen; for instance, 'I've had several managers ringing up to complain about the tone of the circular you sent out last week'
- Pointing out that the shortfall in performance affects you: for example,'... because I've had some problems as a result of the circular ...'
- Pointing out that this shortfall affects the person himself: for instance,'... because I think it will affect the cooperation the other departments will give you'

The idea is not to give masses of detail or long complicated explanation at this point.

Step 4. Here you want assertively to make your specific criticism. 'I' statements are important here, so that the criticism is clearly coming from you and not from some anonymous source. So the following phrases are useful:

- 'I noticed in your return last week that ...'
- 'I'm not happy about the way ...'
- 'As I see it, you are leaving out ...'
- 'I think your report isn't ...'

Such phrases are in contrast to the 'It has been noticed ...' variety. They also contrast with the blaming phrases, which emphasize the *you* ('You really should have adopted a more conciliatory tone in the circular you sent out last week').

It helps if you keep your criticism short and clear to start with. After that you may want to discuss the effect that the shortfall in performance is having. If you mentioned this briefly in Step 3, then you could explore it in more detail here; for instance, 'I think some of the words you have used will alienate some of the managers and make them less willing to cooperate.'

Apart from the above examples, the type of assertion you use at this stage will depend on the circumstances, and whether you have raised this particular issue before with that person. If it is the first time, you can use a basic assertion. If you know that the person is under a lot of pressure at the moment and you want them to know that you recognize this, then an empathetic assertion would be appropriate. Discrepancy and negative feelings are higher-level assertions and are best used when you have raised this particular issue before but the desired change in performance has not been made.

It is usually less effective if you make a lot of criticisms at the same time. There is a strict limit on how many changes anyone can work on at any one time. One is enough, two is plenty, and three is the absolute maximum.

The crucial nonverbal behaviours when giving criticism are eye contact and tone of voice. Too little eye contact and the other person will sense you are having difficulty raising the issue and therefore find it easier to ignore or disagree with what you say. Too much (in the form of glaring) will be seen as aggressive. The voice needs to be matter of fact and not blaming or accusing.

Step 5. This is concerned with getting *agreement* to your criticism. This is vital before you can go on and agree (in Step 6) what changes to make. Responsive assertion will be the predominant behaviour here—you are asking questions to find out if the other person really agrees with your criticism. If not, they may have valid reasons for seeing it differently. If the person agrees, you will probably want to find out why the shortfall in performance has occurred. So Step 5 gives you opportunity to uncover information that may be new to you. This may mean you need to modify your criticism or even withdraw it. It is aggressive to carry on pursuing your original criticism in the face of such new information.

At this stage you may also discover that the other person is not clear on the standards of performance you expect from them in this part of their job.

93

If this happens, it is assertive to acknowledge your own shortfall here. You would then want to make clear what you expect and to get agreement that such standards are realistic. Pursuing your criticism in such situations again would be aggressive; we do not believe you have the *right* to criticize a person's performance if you have not made your expectations clear to them beforehand.

Step 6. This is where you encourage the other person to come up with suggestions to bring about that change. Again, responsive assertion is the major behaviour ('What ideas do you have ...?'). You may need to make some suggestions yourself if the other person is having difficulty in seeing how the change could be made. If you do this with someone who tends to behave nonassertively, it is useful to make the suggestion in a responsive form ('How about trying to ...?' or 'Would it work if you ...?'). This increases the chances of bringing out into the open any difficulties that the other person may have in implementing these suggestions. By the way, the suggestions that arise may well be about *you* making changes—for instance, in the way you schedule the work.

Step 7. Here you summarize what has been agreed. All too often, people go away clear on what they are *not* going to do, but not so clear on what they *are* going to do. So from the suggestions considered, decide which ones are to be actioned. This last step is crucial if the other person is to leave the conversation clear on the changes that they or you will be making. If you close with a statement about how and when you will monitor and review the success of the changes, then the other person is more likely to take the issue seriously.

In conclusion, the above guidelines are meant to be used flexibly. So, for instance, if one of your staff is not completing part of a monthly return correctly, you may not need to go through Steps 6 and 7; you just make your criticism, ask them to do X rather than Y, and check that they understand and agree.

Following these guidelines makes it less likely that the other person will become aggressive or nonassertive. Nonassertion is undesirable because the other person will be holding back from stating their views and airing their doubts. This may result in their *apparently* agreeing to do something differently, but then quietly going back to their old ways once your discussion is over. If you suspect the other person *will* become aggressive or nonassertive, Chapters 9 and 10 deal with how to maintain your assertion.

We have talked so far in this chapter about how to *give* criticism assertively. It also requires skill to *receive* criticism assertively, so the next section looks at this area.

Receiving criticism assertively

No doubt you have been on the receiving end of criticism that you felt was not justified, or, if it was justified, was given aggressively. Either way, you may have responded aggressively or nonassertively. It would be wonderful if everyone made their criticism to you assertively, but this is probably unrealistic! So this section is aimed at helping you respond assertively to criticism, whether it is given assertively, aggressively, or nonassertively.

RIGHTS IN RECEIVING CRITICISM

The first issue to consider is that of rights. If you do not accept that the other person has the right to criticize your performance, then, however they go about it, you will see their behaviour as aggressive. If you accept they have the right, you will want them also to accept *your* rights in this situation—not to be put down, or made to look small or be subjected to personal attacks, and for the criticism to be made in private rather than in front of colleagues.

INNER DIALOGUES

The inner dialogues you have also affect the way you respond to the criticism. Examples of faulty ones are; 'Oh dear, that's another clanger, I'm really bodging this up' or 'He's at it again, always nit-picking, always got to find something wrong'. The former leads you into behaving nonassertively, where you may become over-apologetic or start putting yourself down. The latter pushes you into aggression, because you mentally dismiss what may be valid criticisms before they are even made. So, turn any faulty dialogues you may have into sound ones. For instance: 'I may have made a mistake but not necessarily a complete bodge', or 'The criticism may be a personal attack. I can dig behind that, I can learn from criticism.'

HINTS FOR RECEIVING CRITICISM

Unclear criticism

If you are not clear exactly what the criticism is, you can ask the other person for clarification and for them if possible to give you an example. It is important to do this assertively and not in a challenging way that will be heard as 'go on, I bet you can't think of an example to back up your charge'. Both basic assertions (especially the 'I' statements part) and responsive assertions are useful here. For example: 'I'd find it helpful Pete, if you could give me some examples of what you mean', or 'What sort of thing were you thinking of?' or 'Can you give me some specific instances/examples, Steve?'

Personal attack

If the criticism is made in the form of a personal attack, try and separate in your mind the content (which may be valid) from the way it is given. If such personal attacks have happened before and you want to bring your unease about this to the other person's attention, you can say things like 'I accept

95

that your criticism may be valid, Laura. However, I'd prefer it if you made it less of a personal attack.'

You disagree with the criticism
If you do not accept the criticism, then it is assertive to say so. 'I' statements are important in keeping the interaction on an assertive/assertive level. ('As *I* see it, the ...')

No agreement on future changes
As it is in your interest that suggestions are agreed for the future, you can take the initiative in this area, if the other person appears content to end the interaction before this has been done.

Nonverbal behaviour
Throughout the interaction it is important to maintain steady eye contact. You also need to keep your voice up rather than letting it sink as if you are being deflated. Something else to avoid is letting your voice get high-pitched ('You never told me *that*!'). These suggest that you are on the defensive. Your assertion encourages assertion in the other person.

By following these hints and guidelines you can become more assertive in giving and receiving criticism. Then, like praise, it will become much more an everyday event, carried out in a matter-of-fact way and causing fewer ripples.

8. How others influence you

So far in the book we have concentrated on developing skills for behaving assertively in various situations. However, we recognize that this assertiveness could well break down when 'the going gets rough'—when other people behave aggressively or nonassertively towards you. So the emphasis in these next three chapters is on how you can remain assertive in the light of their aggression and nonassertion. We start the process in this chapter by looking at how other people's behaviour (in the form of ass, agg, or na) influences you. We do this by following through a detailed example. In the following two chapters we show how to handle other people's aggression and nonassertion respectively.

What we mean by influence

It is inevitable when you are interacting with others, whether at work or in your social life, that you will try to influence them. In turn they will try to influence you. We define 'influencing' quite simply as having an effect upon someone. This could mean having an effect on what someone thinks, feels, says, or does. Some of the influence exercised between people is *not legitimate* as far as assertiveness is concerned, because it violates assertive rights. Thus it is not assertive to influence people in any matters—their likes, dislikes, opinions, interests, decisions, actions—that do *not affect* you, but it is a legitimate part of assertiveness to give yourself the right to influence people in matters that do affect you. Alongside this, there is the responsibility of influencing people 'openly': by being assertive rather than aggressive or nonassertive. In addition, it is legitimate to give people the right to influence you in matters that affect them. Unfortunately, they will not always do this assertively but will sometimes use aggression or nonassertion. Later we look at the effects of these three forms of influence on you.

THE TWO ELEMENTS OF INFLUENCE
Other people have two strings to their bow when it comes to influencing you.

- They have the facts, opinions, and suggestions they put forward (we will call these the *content*)
- They have the *way* they put these facts, opinions, and suggestions forward (we call this the *behaviour*)

The following example illustrates what we mean by these two elements.
In a meeting you put forward a suggestion on changes to the maintenance

schedule and a colleague, Kate, says, in a matter-of-fact tone: 'If you do that, breakdowns will increase and it will be more difficult for us to hit the production targets.'

Here, Kate is using the *content*—the facts and opinions—as her primary means of influencing you. Now suppose that, instead of the above reply, Kate had raised her voice and said: 'Oh come on, that's nonsense and you know it. If you do that breakdowns will go through the roof and we'll never hit target.'

Here Kate would be using the *behaviour* (aggression) as her primary means of influencing you. We are concerned in this chapter with the way others use the *behaviours* of aggression, nonassertion and assertion to influence you. We consider the effect of these behaviours on you by following through an example of decision making. We have chosen decision making because this is an area in which others are particularly keen to influence you.

How aggression from others influences you

Let us assume that, after weighing up all the facts and sounding out the people affected, you have decided to make changes to the organization structure of two of the departments that come under your control. You recognize that, whatever decisions you come to, you will not please everyone. You are now at the point of presenting the proposed changes to the staff of these departments.

After your initial presentation of these changes, Norman (a member of staff who has long been a thorn in your flesh) challenges your statement about increased efficiency coming from the reorganization. He does this pretty aggressively, and goes on to point out a couple of problems in making the proposed changes work. He ends up by making a sarcastic reference to some of the other changes you have made.

Unless you are practised at assertively handling aggression, Norman's aggressive behaviour is likely to influence you along one of two routes—nonassertion or aggression. Roughly what happens is this. The emotional overtone of Norman's aggression hooks your own emotions. This happens either because you have not intervened in your *thinking process*, or because you have intervened with a *faulty inner dialogue*. Your own feelings that come to the fore are negative ones, which lead you either into nonassertion or into aggression. Figure 8.1 illustrates this.

We will examine each of the two routes in turn.

WHEN YOU RESPOND NONASSERTIVELY

If you feel embarrassed by Norman's attack in front of a group of your staff, then you may behave nonassertively perhaps by going too far to placate him. To do this you might change your proposals on the reorganization, so that

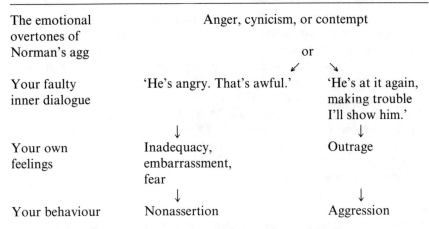

The emotional overtones of Norman's agg — Anger, cynicism, or contempt

or

Your faulty inner dialogue — 'He's angry. That's awful.' — 'He's at it again, making trouble I'll show him.'

Your own feelings — Inadequacy, embarrassment, fear — Outrage

Your behaviour — Nonassertion — Aggression

Figure 8.1   **How the other person's aggression affects you**

they now meet his needs, but not necessarily yours. When this happens, you are making the changes not because of the content of what he says—the problems he raises—but because of the behaviour he uses. When this occurs, *Norman's attempt to influence you to change your decision has been successful.* The important thing to note is that the emotional overtones of the other person's behaviour have lead you into *countering* that behaviour with emotional behaviour of your own (in this case, nonassertion). When this happens, the *content of the behaviour often gets overlooked.* So in the above example the problems Norman raised may or may not be valid but, because your energy goes into countering his behaviour, you may not examine the content very much.

So, in addition to influencing you to change the decision, the other person has also *influenced you to change your behaviour*—from assertion to nonassertion. He is beginning to control your behaviour as well as the decisions you take.

WHEN YOU RESPOND AGGRESSIVELY

If you feel yourself 'bristling' during Norman's attack, then you will most probably respond aggressively. One way to do this is to make a personal attack upon Norman. Another is to make it clear to Norman that you have no intention of changing your proposals, whatever he or anyone else says. Either of these responses will tend to deter any other member of your staff from identifying any potential problems with your proposed changes.

In responding in this way you have again put your energy into countering Norman's behaviour. You are responding to his aggressive behaviour with aggression. But this time his attempt to *influence you to change your decision is unsuccessful.* However, because his aggressive behaviour has hooked your aggression, he *has been successful in influencing you to change your behaviour*. With you putting your energy into countering his behaviour, you are in danger of giving little or no attention to the validity of the content of his contribution. Thus, you may be lumbering yourself with an organizational structure that has real problems associated with it.

This problem of overlooking the content is compounded by the fact that, when a person is being aggressive, he is likely to exaggerate and make extreme statements. So if Norman said something about the proposed changes causing *enormous* problems, then you would see this as an exaggeration. You can easily overlook the valid point behind the exaggeration—that there may well be *some* problems to be ironed out.

IN SUMMARY

Other people's aggression may or may not be successful in influencing you to change a decision you have taken. However, it will certainly influence your behaviour, and start to control it, unless you can maintain your assertion in the face of this aggression. In the next chapter we give some guidelines on how to do this.

How nonassertion from others influences you

You may well have experienced people using aggression to influence you. You may not be so aware that others use nonassertion to the same end. Nonassertion is less dramatic, and less apparent, than aggression. Nevertheless (or maybe because of this!) it can be just as effective in influencing you. Let us return to our example from the previous section, where you have made a decision about organizational changes. Instead of Norman being aggressive, you have a colleague of his, Don, behaving nonassertively when you ask him for his view of the proposed changes. He says something like: 'Well, we do have a lot on at the moment . . . and, er, these changes are bound to take up some of our time. But I suppose we'll try and manage somehow.'

Again, *unless you are practised at responding assertively to nonassertion*, then Don's nonassertion will influence you to respond in one of two ways: nonassertively or aggressively. What happens here is that the overtones of Don's behaviour contain a sort of 'emotional blackmail'. It doesn't 'hit you as hard' as aggressive emotion. Nevertheless, it may be just as effective in hooking your own feelings, which in turn lead you to behave nonassertively or aggressively. We illustrate how this happens in Figure 8.2. We will explore each of these two alternatives in more detail.

WHEN YOU RESPOND NONASSERTIVELY

If you start feeling guilty for making additional demands upon Don, this is because his nonassertion has led you to have a faulty inner dialogue. What

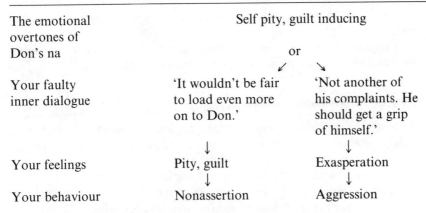

The emotional overtones of Don's na	Self pity, guilt inducing	
	or	
Your faulty inner dialogue	'It wouldn't be fair to load even more on to Don.'	'Not another of his complaints. He should get a grip of himself.'
Your feelings	Pity, guilt	Exasperation
Your behaviour	Nonassertion	Aggression

Figure 8.2   **How the other person's nonassertion affects you**

you say to yourself and what you feel, will lead you to behave nonassertively. For instance, you might put off the date for implementing the changes in Don's section with the result that your needs are no longer met. So *Don's behaviour, his nonassertion—rather than the content of his statement—has influenced you to change the decision.*

In addition, Don's *nonassertion has influenced you to change your behaviour,* from assertion to nonassertion. You are moving away from controlling your own behaviour.

As with responding to aggression, when you put energy into countering the emotions associated with the other person's nonassertion you tend to give less attention to the content of the statement. So in the example you may not check the validity of Don's problems or whether they can be overcome without major changes to your decision.

WHEN YOU RESPOND AGGRESSIVELY
This can come about because your faulty inner dialogue leads you to feel exasperated with Don's nonassertion. For instance, you may see his statement about the workload as just one more in a long line of non-assertive complaints from him. Then your exasperation will spill over into aggressive retorts like: 'Don, isn't it about time you got on top of things?'

When this occurs you are ceasing to listen to the content of Don's contribution to see if it is valid, and you are again responding to his behaviour. If there is a real problem with implementing the required changes while coping with the heavy workload, then you have failed to pick it up.

So Don's attempt to influence you with nonassertion to change the decision has failed. But he has influenced you to change your behaviour, from assertion to aggression—thus removing some of your control over yourself.

In Chapter 10 we give some hints for responding assertively to nonassertion. But now we will look at assertion influencing you.

How assertion from others influences you

Following through our previous example, let us consider how Penny, another member of staff, might influence you. She says: 'I believe on the whole the changes will improve overall efficiency. However, I see a real problem in meeting some of the proposed implementation dates.'

It is likely that you will say to yourself, 'Ah, that seems a reasonable point.' This sound inner dialogue and her assertive behaviour will lead you to feel calm about the whole thing and you are likely to respond along the following lines: 'Why is that, Penny?'

When this happens, you are concentrating upon the content of Penny's contribution and trying to get more facts and information, in order to be able to decide if, and how, the implementation dates can be met. In the light of the information that comes out you will be able to take a more objective rather than emotional decision about whether to modify any of the implementation dates.

This comes about because there are no negative feeling accompanying Penny's behaviour, so it makes it easier for you to conduct the discussion on an assertive–assertive level. We summarize this in Figure 8.3.

Penny may or may not be successful in influencing you to change the decision. This will not matter. What matters is that, if the decision is changed or if it remains unaltered, *this will be in the light of the content of what the other person says.*

Before moving on to handle aggression and nonassertion in Chapters 9 and 10, we would like to examine a particularly powerful way in which people can influence you.

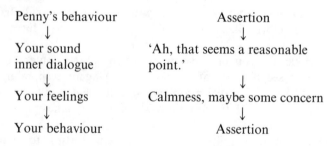

Figure 8.3   How assertion affects you

How people influence you through their past behaviour

In addition to people influencing you through their present behaviour of aggression, nonassertion and assertion, *people can also influence you through their past behaviour*. We will again refer to decision making in order to demonstrate this. In the previous examples all the attempts to influence you occurred *after* you made your decision. This time we will look at how people can influence you *before* you make a decision.

Of course, you may be well aware of people trying to influence you before you make a decision—when they come to you 'lobbying' when you go to them collecting information, say, about alternatives. You probably realize that people usually have more to gain by influencing you before you make a decision. They can influence you to decide on one particular alternative as opposed to another; whereas, after you have made a decision, their influence is usually restricted to getting modifications to the alternative you have chosen.

What you may not be so conscious of is that people can influence you before you even talk to anyone—*while you are still thinking about a decision*. Let us give an example of this.

Suppose in the past you have been on the end of aggression from a colleague, Jane, when you have taken a decision that was not to her liking. Then you may have a faulty dialogue at work along the lines of 'I would really like to make that change, but if I do Jane will get really annoyed. I don't want to upset her again. It's a pity, but I think I had better hold fire on that.'

The interesting point here is that Jane does not need to *behave* aggressively towards you this time round. She is influencing you successfully through the faulty inner dialogue you are carrying around as the result of past experiences.

Table 8.1 gives some examples of faulty dialogues based upon experiences

Table 8.1   Faulty dialogues about decision making, based on people's past behaviour

Faulty inner dialogues

1. They'll never stand for it. If I go ahead and do that I'll be really unpopular. That would be terrible.
2. Who do they think they are, always trying to veto my decisions? I'm the manager. They'll do what I decide.
3. It wouldn't be fair to Ian if I decide to make changes now. He won't say so but I know he'll be worried.
4. You can't be liked and get things done in this job. Making tough decisions is what I'm paid for.

103

of people's past reaction. Faulty dialogues 1 and 3 will lead you to behave nonassertively; 2 and 4 will lead you to behave aggressively.

Summary

When people influence you, or have influenced you in the past with assertion it makes it easier for you to respond assertively to them. At these times you can concentrate on the content of their behaviour. When people influence you, or have influenced you in the past with aggression or nonassertion, it makes it more difficult for you to respond assertively. This is because the negative feelings accompanying their behaviours get in the way of the content.

In Chapters 9 and 10 we show how to handle aggression and nonassertion assertively. This means that you will be more likely to retain control of your behaviour. In addition, you will be influenced only by the validity of the content of what the other person says.

9. Handling aggression from others

You are not alone if you find it difficult to cope with aggression from others. Many people feel that highly aggressive exchanges leave them emotionally drained and saying to themselves: 'There must be a better way of handling it.' If you can remember saying things like this to yourself, it is probable that when faced with aggression your response was to be aggressive or nonassertive. We said in Chapter 8 that it is very easy for your response to aggression to go in one of these two ways and we explained how these two responses result from other people *succeeding* in influencing your *behaviour* with their aggression.

In this chapter we give you some guidelines on responding assertively to aggression and thus retaining control of your own behaviour. We will begin by a brief recap of some of the different levels of aggression, some of which we have mentioned in earlier chapters.

Different levels of aggression

We find it useful to draw a distinction between higher levels of aggression and lower levels of aggression.

HIGHER-LEVEL ASSERTION

This usually takes the form of *personal attacks*, as shown in these examples:

- 'That's not true and you jolly well know it!'
- 'You've been making life difficult for me whenever you've had the slightest chance. I'm really sick of it!'
- 'That's just typical of you! I might have known you'd come up with another tin pot scheme. Just like the last time ... '

Personal attacks indicate that people are personalizing the differences that exist between themselves and others. So, instead of attacking the issue, they attack the person. People who are high on aggression are fond of using these behaviours because they fit in with their beliefs about other people being out to get them and win at their expense.

LOWER-LEVEL AGGRESSION

This can take various forms, some of which are:

		Comments
Sarcasm	'What's this masterpiece, then?'	These can become very 'clever' and cutting
Blaming	'It's all engineering's fault.'	Often contain exaggerations
Dismissing the person/their statement	Dismissive hand gesture; sometimes a sneer 'No. That won't work.'	May show contempt
Patronizing	'It won't be all that bad once you get going. You'll see.'	Treating the other person like a child, condescending

This lower level can also consist of: not listening to you, or hogging the conversation.

Later in the chapter we have guidelines for handling the higher level of aggression, and an exercise for dealing with the lower levels. In the next section we start to cross the barriers that exist between previous ways of handling aggression and future assertive ways.

Overcoming barriers to responding assertively

We believe that the most useful way to improve your handling of other people's aggression is to start with someone who has previously been aggressive to you and whom you think is likely to be aggressive in the future. There are probably a number of *barriers* preventing you from changing the way you handle aggression from this person—most notably your inner dialogue and your feelings. We suggest you begin by tackling these barriers right now.

To start with, recall one or two occasions when you did not handle an aggressive attack from this person as well as you would have liked. (You may have behaved nonassertively, perhaps becoming apologetic or going on the defensive. Or you may have used aggression, saying things you later regretted.) Make a note of your inner dialogues—the things you are saying to yourself—as you think back to the previous incidents and think forward to future aggressive attacks from this person. Also take note of the feelings you experience.

The vital thing in removing any barriers of this sort is to change any faulty dialogues into sound ones and to check that your feelings are productive rather than negative. Here are some examples of the sort of thing you might come up with.

IF YOU PREVIOUSLY USED AGGRESSION

Inner dialogue	*Type*	*You feel*	*Leading to*
'I really made a fool of myself then. Whatever must the others think of me now? I'd better keep quiet next time.'	Faulty	Embarrassment, guilt, or shame	Future nonassertion

106

Inner dialogue	Type	You feel	Leading to
'I did get a bit steamed up there but he asked for it. I'll get mad again if he behaves like that.'	Faulty	Justified	Future aggression
'I'm disappointed I let myself get into that slanging match. Next time he behaves like that I'll count to 10 before responding.'	Sound	Disappointment mixed with confidence	Future assertion

IF YOU PREVIOUSLY USED NONASSERTION

Inner dialogue	Type	You feel	Leading to
'I really missed out there, but I'll be ready for her next time. I'll show her.'	Faulty	Frustration, anger	Future aggression
'There's no need for her to be so abrasive. Still, she's the manager and I don't suppose there's much I can do about the way she behaves.'	Faulty	Helplessness, self-pity, or hurt	Future nonassertion
'I needn't have been so cowed even if she is the manager. Next time she's aggressive I can stand up to her.'	Sound	Concern, some confidence	Future assertion

In order to help you get on board with a sound inner dialogue we would like to say a bit more about other people's emotional overtones that accompany their aggression. (You may recall that in Chapter 8 we said these emotional overtones hook your own negative feelings, leading you to behave aggressively or nonassertively.) Two of the feelings that often lie behind people's aggression are anger and frustration. These are feelings that many people never learn to deal with effectively. They learn to suppress them or to give vent to them, and this latter sometimes means projecting them on to other people. So when a colleague expressed anger against you he may well be angry with *himself*. He is projecting it on to *you*. He might say things like 'You make me furious when you don't follow the laid down procedure'; whereas he is actually frustrated at himself because he has not achieved much today. At other times people may feel angry with *someone else* whom they cannot express their anger to. If you happen to be around at the time they may take this anger out on you.

107

If you have developed a sound inner dialogue and have productive feelings, you have overcome two barriers to making changes in the way you handle aggression from others. Also, these inner dialogues will help you to trigger off sound inner dialogues *during* an aggressive attack from someone. We refer to these later in the next section. Let us now look at ways of maintaining your assertion in the face of aggression.

Responding assertively to aggression from others

The aim of handling other people's aggression is *to get the interaction on to an assertive–assertive level*, so that *issues are dealt with and you feel OK about the interaction afterwards*. In addition, handling aggression with assertion reduces the chances of aggression recurring from that person in future.

SOME GUIDELINES FOR HANDLING AGGRESSION FROM OTHERS
In Figure 9.1 we introduce some guidelines for maintaining your assertion in the face of other people's aggression. The specific aim is to *defuse the*

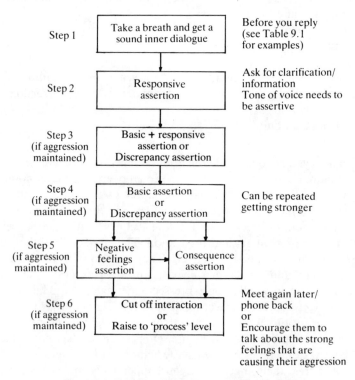

Figure 9.1 Guidelines for handling aggression from others

aggression in the other person. The guidelines consist of a number of steps that you can take in standing your ground in the face of aggression.

The first step is crucial. If you can get a sound inner dialogue going at this stage, it increases considerably your chances of responding assertively. Just 'counting to three' buys you crucial seconds to do this. In addition, using starter words like 'Well . . . ' or 'OK, . . . ' buys you a few more split seconds. These few seconds are helpful to you whether you tend to behave nonassertively or aggressively in the face of aggression.

Table 9.1 gives examples of some of the faulty split-second inner dialogues you could have in the face of aggression, along with a useful sound inner dialogue to develop.

EXAMPLE OF THE GUIDELINES AT WORK

You are meeting with another manager (John), when he makes the following personal attack upon you. He says 'This is *typical* of the way *your* department has ignored our requests since *you* took over.'

Given that you resist the temptation to hit back in kind or become nonassertive, what sort of things could you say, that would be in line with the guidelines for responding assertively. There are of course many possibilities. Below we have given one possible route you might go down, given that John keeps behaving aggressively towards you. We come in at Step 2 and concentrate upon your responses.

Table 9.1   Split-second inner dialogues

Inner dialogue	Feelings	Behaviour
Faulty		
• Who does he think he is?	Anger	Aggression
• I wish she'd keep her voice down. Everybody's watching.	Embarrassment; guilt	Nonassertion
• I made a stupid mistake but he's no right to go on like this.	Frustration; anger	Aggression
• How could she accuse me of doing that deliberately?	Hurt	Nonassertion
• I'd better go along with what he's saying. Otherwise he'll get out of control and anything could happen.	Fear	Nonassertion
Sound		
• I can handle this.	Concern; calmness	Assertion
• I can stay calm.	confidence	

YOU		JOHN
Step 2 *Responsive*	'What makes you say that, John?'	
		Aggression maintained
Step 3 *Basic and responsive*	'I don't believe we have ignored your requests, John, but I'd like to hear why you feel we have.'	
	or	
Empathetic	'I recognize your strong feelings on this, John. However, I do see it differently in that ... '	
		Aggression maintained
Step 4 *Basic*	'I see it differently, John.'	
	or	
Discrepancy	'On the one hand you say you want to improve relations between our departments, but on the other you're saying things that work against that. Now, let's look at what the problems are.'	
		Aggression maintained
Step 5 *Negative feelings*	'John, I feel annoyed when you make statements like the one earlier. It makes it more difficult for us to cooperate. I'd like us to sort out together the problems we have.'	
	or	
Consequence	'John, if you continue in this way, I won't be prepared to put any more effort into sorting out these problems. Now I'd rather we did sort them out.'	
		Aggression maintained
Step 6 *Cut off interaction*	'I'd like to leave the issue there for now. I think we'd do better to talk about it later.'	

110

	or
Raise to process level	'I don't believe, John, that we're making progress. I think we need to stop now and look at why we are having these disagreements.'

NOTES ON USING THE GUIDELINES

We see the guidelines as a series of options available to you, while behaving assertively in the face of aggression. They are not intended as a rigid set of rules, so you may for example want to ask a series of questions in Step 2 to find out what the specific problem is. You may, of course, succeed in defusing the aggression at this stage. On the other hand you may want sometimes to move quickly to cutting off the interaction.

A useful rule of thumb is only to step up your assertion if the other person continues to behave aggressively. We have found that much aggression can be defused at the lower levels of Steps 2 and 3, especially if your initial response is appropriately assertive. The knowledge that you do have higher level options available if you choose to use them can increase your confidence and help you to behave with firmer assertiveness at the lower levels.

We would now like to add some notes to each of the steps.

Step 2

Aggression often comes to you as a bolt from the blue, for example when someone rings you up or bursts into your office. When this occurs it is crucial to be clear what the other person is saying and why they are saying it. Particularly where someone is extremely aggressive, the words often come out very quickly and may not even be coherent to you. Responsive assertions in the form of those listed below are necessary to reach the point where you have enough information to be able to respond assertively about the problem or issue.

Asking for information	'When did this happen, Jenny?' 'Why do you say that, Steve?' 'What's actually happened?' 'Can you give me some specific examples, Dave?'
Asking for clarification	'What do you mean by ...?' 'When you say ..., what were you thinking of?'
Checking your understanding	'So have I got it right; What you're saying is ...?' 'Can I just check that what you're saying is ...?'

It is crucial, of course, that you ask these questions assertively, in particular keeping your voice up and evenly paced. Slowing your response down may encourage the other person to slow down and to start giving you some facts to work on. Asking questions, and listening to the responses, shows the

111

aggressor that you are open-minded at this stage. Allowing the other person to talk also helps them to relax slightly. Sometimes they may be so pent-up that you are unable to get a word in even to ask a question. In this case it is often better to let them get it off their chests. Once this has happened the exchange stands a better chance of becoming an assertive–assertive one.

If this does not happen and the other person maintains their aggression in response to your questions, then you can try Step 3 of the guidelines.

Step 3

At this stage you are saying more about *where you stand* on the issue under discussion. At the same time, both options (basic, and responsive or empathetic) show you are interested in the other person's position. The aggressor may well feel at this stage that they are getting through to you, even if your assertion shows them that your position is still different from theirs. This does not necessarily stop them trying to influence you, but it does make it more likely that they will now feel able to try and influence you through what they have to *say*, rather than the *way they say it*. If this happens, their behaviour will become more assertive and less aggressive.

The behaviours in Steps 2 and 3 do form a powerful combination. It is often more difficult for people to go on being aggressive to someone who is being assertive in this way. But why not test this out for yourself? Read the previous example and see how difficult you find it to maintain your aggression in the light of the assertive statements in Steps 2 and 3.

Step 4

You step up your assertion at this stage if the other person maintains their aggression in spite of your efforts at Steps 2 and 3. Here you increase the emphasis upon *your position*.

The first option is a basic assertion on its own. This may be a restatement of your position, or it may be different from earlier statements in that it takes account of new information contained in the other person's most recent contribution. In order to give strength to a restatement of your position it is useful to slow it down and give emphasis to key words. A short, firm, basic assertion can be particularly useful if the other person has ignored your earlier statements where you are stating that you see it differently.

Another alternative at this stage is to use discrepancy assertion, particularly if you think past agreements are being broken or if the other person's behaviour is out of line with their words.

Step 5

If you have worked at being assertive, with no change in the other person's aggression, you may start to experience strong feelings of frustration, resentment or annoyance. As we have said earlier such feelings can become a

112

barrier to your own assertion. Hence, it would be important to express these feelings to the other person.

Alternatively, you feel you have reached the point where a consequence assertion would be appropriate. A useful consequence at this stage, is to say that you will end the discussion unless the other person changes their behaviour e.g. 'Ray, if you continue to shout in this way, I shall put the phone down and ring you back later.' As with all consequence assertions, it is crucial to say it in a matter-of-fact way.

Whether you use negative feelings or consequence assertion, the other person will see that you mean business at this stage, and it may well lead to a 'grudging' assertion from them.

Step 6

If all your efforts so far have failed, you might be saying to yourself 'Well, that's it. I've tried everything else, now I can be aggressive without feeling bad about it!' Before your faulty dialogue leads you into aggression, there are two more options open to you.

One is to cut off the interaction. You may already have warned the other person of this in the previous step (as we illustrated with the consequence assertion above). In any case a simple statement along the following lines will be sufficient at this point: 'I don't feel that we are making progress. I'd like us to meet tomorrow when we have had time to think about the problem'; or 'I am not prepared to continue in this way. Let's ... '.

Using negative feelings or consequence assertion, or cutting off your interaction in this way, alerts the other person to the effect of their behaviour. They may not have thought too much about this before. Also, these options make it clear that you are not prepared to take their maintained aggression.

The second option is what we call 'raising to the process level'. This is particularly useful when similar incidents keep recurring. What you do is to put aside the issue you are discussing (or arguing about!) and encourage the other person to talk about the underlying issue or feelings that are leading them to behave aggressively towards you. An example of this is the difficulties Linda (the manager) was having with one of her staff (Gordon). Linda had been doing her present job for about three months. During this time she had found Gordon very aggressive towards her. The issues they disagreed over did not seem that important as far as Linda could see, and Gordon appeared very reluctant to move an inch, even when Linda made it clear she was prepared to compromise. Linda sensed that Gordon had strong feelings of resentment towards her and that it was probably because she got the job rather than him. Linda decided to raise this the next time Gordon and she got locked into a lengthy aggressive exchange. So, after arguing over a particular procedure for about 20 minutes, Linda said: 'Gordon, over the last three months we have spent a lot of time arguing over various issues. I'd like to be clearer why this has happened. Can we forget the procedure for the moment and talk about why we have these long arguments?'

Such an approach can be successful in that Gordon may start talking about his underlying feelings. If he does, Linda will become clearer on what these feelings are, and Gordon may move towards recognizing and acknowledging them. This opens the door to their improving the relationship in the future.

Coping with 'everyday put-downs'

The memory of exchanges where there is sustained aggression may stick with you for quite a while. You may not be so aware of the short one-off, low level aggressive behaviours that come your way. By these we mean comments or questions like:

- 'That's personnel for you'
- 'Haven't you finished that report yet?'

We use the phrase 'everyday put-downs' to describe this form of aggression. Sometimes they stand on their own. Other times they come in the middle of a conversation. They can come in all shapes and sizes. They are aimed at putting you in a 'one-down' position, by undermining your credibility or point scoring at your expense. Such comments may niggle or embarrass you. They need to be dealt with, preferably at the time, otherwise they can eat away at your relationship with the person who makes them.

We distinguish these put-downs from the fun 'banter' that goes on where the comments and jokes are intended and received as humour. Put-downs are not usually 'straight' in the sense that there is often a hidden message behind the words said. For instance the example above 'Haven't you finished that report yet?' By the words and the way they are said, it is clear that this is no straight request for information as to when you will have finished the report. The person making the remark may really be saying to you (and this is the hidden message) 'I think you're taking too long over that report.'

So when you are on the receiving end of these put-downs you need to decide how you are going to handle them. At the moment you may ignore them, even though they irritate (na) or you may come back with a clever retort (agg). The danger of either of these approaches is that you may be encouraging the other person to go on making the put-downs, or you may be missing an opportunity to find out what the hidden message is. While we accept there are occasions when it would be inappropriate to respond to a put-down, we believe that the objective of reducing the number of put-downs is best achieved by responding assertively at the time. As it is low level aggression, it is appropriate initially to use the low level assertions of Steps 2

114

and 3 of our guidelines i.e. responsive, basic and sometimes empathetic. Responsive assertion is particularly useful for getting at any hidden messages.

In the following section, there is an exercise for practising assertive responses to the put-downs you encounter.

EXERCISE FOR COPING WITH PUT-DOWNS

Part One
In Table 9.2 we have listed examples of some of the more common types of

Table 9.2   Exercise: Coping with everyday put-downs

Type of put-down	Example	Your assertive response
Stereotyping you	'That's typical of production/ accountant/sales etc.'	
Insinuating	'I expect you've got plenty of spare time (in your department).'	
Making decisions on your behalf	'What I'd do, if I were you, is spend less time on the detail of your job.'	
Questioning your judgement, values, or beliefs	'Are you really sure he'll be able to do the job?' 'You don't really believe *that* do you?'	
Patronizing	'Well, don't worry yourself about all that, I'll take care of it.'	
Nagging	'How much longer are you going to spend on that report?'	
Inferring you are lying	'Oh, come on, you know that's not how it happened.'	
Making generaliz- ations about your personality	'I think you're far too nice to succeed.'	
Using emotive words to describe your actions	'That was a crazy decision.' 'It was irresponsible of you not to let me know.'	

115

Table 9.3   Possible answers to the put-downs

Example put-down	Possible assertive reply
'That's typical of production/ accountants/sales etc.'	'Jill, I don't believe it's typical. Why do you think it is?'
'I expect you've got plenty of spare time in your department.'	'What makes you say that?'
'What I'd do, if I were you, is spend less time on the detail of your job.'	'I appreciate your concern, Nigel. However, I believe the detail is important.'
'Are you really sure, he'll be able to do the job?'	'I believe he will.'
'You don't really believe *that*, do you?'	'Yes, I do believe that.'
'Well, don't worry yourself about all that. I'll take care of it.'	'I'm not worried about it, but I am concerned. I'm happy to look after it myself.'
'How much longer are you going to spend on that report?'	'Is there a problem on time-scales?' 'Why are you asking?'
'Oh come on, you know that's not how it happened.'	'That certainly is the way I saw it.'
'I think you're far too nice to succeed.'	'What do you mean by nice, George?' 'I don't see it that way.' 'I don't accept you have to be nasty to succeed.'
'That was a crazy decision.'	'I'm not happy with the decision in retrospect, but I don't think it was crazy.'
'It was irresponsible of you not to let me know.'	'I accept that it was a mistake not to let you know, but I would not describe it as irresponsible.'

put-downs (the list is not exhaustive). We suggest you use the list in the following way.

1. Modify the list of examples in any way you like until it corresponds to put-downs that you have encountered in the past.
2. Produce a form of words that you feel happy to use as an assertive

response to each of the put-downs. (Basic, responsive or empathetic assertions are likely to be the most useful.)

3. Compare your responses with the ones we have suggested in Table 9.3. If they are different it does not mean they are wrong, as there are many different assertive responses you can make to each put-down. The important thing is that a response should be assertive, hence *showing that you will not let the put-down succeed.* This decreases the chances that the other person will make such put-downs in the future.

Part Two
We now suggest you practise making your responses in an assertive way. You can do this on your own, although you will probably have more fun and learn more if you invite someone to join you. Your 'partner' does not have to know much about assertiveness as long as he or she can make the put-downs to you in the mildly aggressive manner you are familiar with. If you are working with someone else you need to give them the list of examples and ask them to say the put-downs to you in *random* order. You then respond with the words you decided on in Part One, or with similar ones. If you are on your own, just practise saying the responses out loud to yourself. (It's OK to talk to yourself!) Either way, take your time in saying your responses. Because the put-downs often come rapidly, 'out of the blue', you may think you have to react and respond quickly. But this can actually make your assertion less effective.

Summary

Coping assertively with aggression is demanding. However, if you recognize that you have a number of options then this can give you confidence. Questions are often crucial to give you time and to get at the facts or the hidden messages. If you combine them with slowing down your own responses, then you stand a good chance of handling the next aggression that comes your way that bit more effectively.

10. Handling nonassertion from others

In Chapter 8 we said that nonassertion from other people can influence your own behaviour. We explained how the emotions accompanying the other person's nonassertion hook your own feelings, which in turn can move you away from assertion into nonassertion or aggression, depending on which feelings you have. In addition, we said that you may change your mind—about a decision, an opinion, or a course of action—not so much because you are responding to the content of what the person says, but because you are responding to the nonassertive behaviour itself. Whether the nonassertion influences you to change your mind or not, the other person still gets something of what they want. They may have led you to feel sorry or guilty on their behalf, which can be comforting and rewarding to them. Or they may have aroused your anger, irritation, or frustration, which in turn will lead them to feel hurt or self-pity, both of which can be comforting to them and thus reinforcing. All this 'emotional blackmail' is not only pretty unhealthy, but it also makes it difficult for you to have open, straightforward dealings with a person behaving non-assertively.

In a sense there is a temptation to leave people to their own devices when they behave nonassertively—because they are not necessarily violating your rights, as people are when they behave aggressively. If nonassertion had *no* effect on you, then this would certainly be one way of handling it. But as we have already said, nonassertion affects your own feelings and behaviour, and can affect the outcome of a situation (we give more examples of this later in the chapter). In addition, the definition of assertiveness includes 'not violating the rights, not ignoring the needs, wants and opinions of others.' So in order for you to be assertive, you need *to know* what these needs, wants and opinions are—sometimes difficult when people are nonassertive about expressing them!

Therefore, in this chapter we look at how to handle nonassertion assertively, so that you retain control over your own feelings and behaviour while also moving the other person some way towards behaving more assertively in return. We explore different forms of nonassertion and some ways of responding assertively to them.

Different forms of nonassertion

In Table 10.1 we look more closely at some of the different forms of nonassertion that you may come into contact with at work. (Some of these we have mentioned in earlier chapters.)

Table 10.1   A closer look at forms of nonassertion

Form of na	Examples	What might really be going on?
Tentative or reluctant agreement	'Oh, I suppose so.' 'Well it might be OK.' 'Maybe you're right.'	Going along with you because they are unwilling to disagree; wanting to avoid conflict; wanting to please you.
Hinting at or tentatively expressing doubts/difficulties	'I'm not really sure about that.' 'That may be a bit awkward.'	Playing 'safe.' They can then retract the doubt if you get aggressive; or if you behave nonassertively they can then state the doubt in 'safety'.
Stating excuses	'I haven't really got time.' 'I would, only I'm rushed off my feet.' 'I can't really because I have to ...'.	'Time' and 'overwork' are the more common 'smokescreens'. They are putting you off the 'scent' of the real reason, which may be an unstated preference of a lack of ability and/or confidence.
Unwilling to state preferences	'Oh, I don't really mind.' 'Whichever way suits you best.'	Wanting to be helpful or sometimes unwilling to take responsibility. Often have preferences but unwilling to state them—may complain afterwards.
Moaning or complaining —about you	'Oh dear, not another set of figures.' 'Oh no! We've got so much to do.'	Maybe to you directly or just within earshot—trying to make you feel guilty.
—about a third party	'They expect you to do everything all at once.'	Trying to enlist your support. Often unwilling to take direct action—prefer your sympathy instead.
Eliciting praise	'I thought it didn't go too well, what do you think?'	Often don't believe this negative self-assessment, but want you not only to disagree with it but probably to be complimentary.
Seeking confirmation/ permission/approval	'I thought I might ... do you think I should?'	Unwilling to base decisions on their own judgement—maybe about matters that do not affect you. They have your advice to back them up if anything goes wrong. (Not the same as collecting facts about how things might work out, or seeking your reaction to things that affect you.)

119

Table 10.1 *(continued)*

Form of na	*Examples*	*What might really be going on?*
Helplessness and self-pity	'I don't think I'll ever get this lot sorted out. I don't seem to be getting anywhere.' 'What's the use of . . .'.	Seeing themselves as powerless to influence their surroundings/make changes in their own behaviour. Wanting you to feel sorry for their 'plight'. Sometimes to avoid taking action.
Self put-downs	'I'm hopeless at . . .'. 'You know me, I'm bound to get it all wrong.' 'I made a real mess of that presentation.'	There may be a genuine lack of ability and/or confidence, but often expressed as exaggerations, understating capabilities— sometimes to avoid doing something or to avoid criticism (by getting in first); sometimes to elicit a compliment.
Proposals at their own expense	'Would you like me to take that home? I really don't mind.' 'I haven't a lot of time but I can do it in the lunch break.'	Over-helpfulness. Often trying to please you. Sometimes trying to put you in their debt so you'll feel grateful. Sometimes wanting you to feel guilty about them going out of their way in denying their own needs and wants.
Enhancing others at their own expense	'You always seem to get on well using these machines. I'm hopeless at it.' 'She's so calm about handling awkward customers. There's no way I could be like that.'	Wanting to admire or flatter the other person. Negative comparisons sometimes enable the person to avoid criticism or taking on a new or difficult task.

ANOTHER FORM OF NONASSERTION

In the examples in Table 10.1 the nonassertion consists of statements that are tentative, apologetic, or self-demeaning. A rather different, but very common, form of nonassertion is when a person *fails to say anything at all*. Examples of this would be failing to raise an important issue, to state disagreement, or to state wants. When a person keeps quiet like this it may not affect you at the time, but it can often rebound later on. For instance, has the following sort of thing ever happened to you? You were in a meeting where people agreed to submit monthly progress reports. Three of your colleagues clearly supported this idea while a fourth *did not disagree*. At the end of the month four of you produced reports as agreed, but your remaining colleague did not. When you asked them about this you discovered they did not think it was a good idea in the first place!

This form of nonassertion is difficult to detect at the time. However, there may well be some nonverbal clues that can help you to spot this 'silent' nonassertion. Here are some examples:

Lack of eye contact—maybe even 'shifty' sidelong glances
Facial expressions—face puckering or lips pursed indicating doubt
Shuffling body movements ⎫__ indicating a wish to get away, to avoid
Restless hand movements ⎭   potential disagreement

The pattern that emerges with many of these forms of nonassertion is that you are unclear on what the other person really believes, feels, or wants. You may even end up not trusting them; you suspect they say one thing but do another—a particularly effective form of sabotage against you. With all the forms of nonassertion, the person may or may not be aware of their behaviour and its effects on you. What matters though is that *you* are now aware of what *might* be going on. So you are in a better position to handle some of the exchanges you get involved in, some of which might otherwise be quite lengthy and unproductive.

Responding assertively to nonassertion

The aim, when you are responding assertively to nonassertion, is to get the interaction to an ass–ass level. This involves you in retaining control over yourself, first of all.

RETAINING CONTROL OF YOUR FEELINGS

The first step towards this is being *aware* of how the other person's nonassertion can influence your own feelings.

The second step is to have a *sound inner dialogue* with yourself, as follows:

1. If you know *in advance* that you are going to meet with a person who is often nonassertive, you can 'talk to yourself' beforehand. For example:
   'I know Dave is usually over-helpful, making promises he cannot keep. I can get him to be realistic and to state any problems. I need not be fobbed off by unrealistic promises.'
2. If a person has come to you *unexpectedly* and you find yourself having to respond to her nonassertion, then you can take a deep breath and hold a split second inner dialogue. For example:
   'Sue seems to be giving me excuses. I need not let that irritate me. I can get at the real reason.'

BEHAVING ASSERTIVELY IN THE FACE OF NONASSERTION

In Table 10.2 we give some examples of assertive responses to six nonassertive replies. The aim with all of the assertive responses is to get at the issues

121

Table 10.2   Examples of assertive responses to nonassertion

Na reply	Ass response	Comments
1. 'Well ... all right, then.' (*tentative agreement*)	'You seem to be hesitating. 'What's the difficulty?' (*responsive*)	You need to find out if there *is* a problem and *what* it is before you can get a firm commitment.
2. 'That ... er ... may leave me with a bit of a problem.' (*tentatively expressing doubts*)	'What is the problem? Let's see if it can be sorted out.' (*responsive and/or basic*)	This makes it clear that you realize there may be a genuine problem but that it need not get in the way.
3. 'Well, I don't seem to be able to find time to get started on it.' (*stating excuses*)	'Oh, I see. Well, I think there may be a way round that. Is there any other problem Bill?' (*basic or empathetic and responsive*)	Sometimes difficult to distinguish an excuse from a real reason. This response avoids 'red rag' words (like 'excuses' or 'real') that may make him think you are accusing him or lying.
4. 'I haven't a lot of time as I'm out this week and next, but I suppose I can work at home over the weekend.' (*proposals at own expense*)	'I'm glad you mentioned about being out this week and next. Can we look for ways around this so you don't have to work over the weekend?' (*empathetic or basic + responsive*)	This enables you to avoid feeling guilty, sorry, or over-grateful. If there is no way around this and you have to accept the offer simply say 'Thank you, Bill' with no lengthy apologies.
5. 'I'm hopeless at writing reports. I made a real mess of the last one.' (*putting self down*)	'I don't agree you are hopeless at reports. The last one was not good, but I believe you *can* write reports. What specific problems do you have with them?' (*basic and responsive*)	Important to counter his exaggerations with a more realistic assessment—no effusive praise. They give assurance to improve confidence—avoid fatherly 'pep' talks (You'll be all right, no need to worry'). Treating him like a child encourages nonassertion.
6. 'You're very good at writing reports. I seem to find it really slow and time-consuming.' (*enhancing others at own expense*)	'What makes it so slow and time-consuming?' (*responsive*)	This avoids the negative comparison and looks for facts.

and avoid the emotional blackmail of the nonassertion; then, having done this, to get the other person to behave assertively in return. The nonassertions are six of the many possible replies that a person could give in the following situation.

Situation: You have previously mentioned to one of your staff that when his project finishes you would need a report from him within a month of the finish date. The project has not ended, so you want to agree a deadline for the report. You say 'Bill, you know that project report I mentioned, I'd like to have it from you by the end of the month. Is that OK with you?'

Of course, it is sometimes unrealistic to try and get the other person to behave assertively. If you manage to maintain your own assertion and to get them to deal with the issues *less* nonassertively, then this may be as much as you can achieve.

Sometimes the other person may get irritated and behave aggressively. So in the situation on which Table 10.2 is based, after several assertions from you he might say, 'Well, I've already told you, leave it with me.' This can happen because he realizes after a number of assertions from you that you are not playing the game he wants (feeling guilty or sorry for him). Sometimes it can be that he sees a threat in being asked several questions (asking them in matter-of-fact, non-criticizing ways helps to avoid this). If the person does become aggressive, then you can stick to your assertiveness. Remember, '*you have the right to behave assertively*'. A switch from nonassertion to aggression is the 'worst' that can happen to you. In many cases you are just going to be dealing with nonassertion. In itself this can be quite tiring, because in a sense the ball keeps coming back to you, so that you have to keep taking the initiative.

Summary

So in this chapter we have:

- Looked at some different forms of nonassertion
- Suggested some assertive responses you can make to them.
- Stressed that, although it is tempting to 'let sleeping dogs lie', this is undesirable because nonassertion from others leaves you with a number of problems—not least that it makes it more difficult for you to behave assertively.

11. Negotiating acceptable outcomes

In Chapter 4 we gave you some hints for saying 'No' assertively. We would now like to return to this theme to explore the area of negotiating. If you are behaving assertively you will need and want to say 'No' in certain situations. In other situations you or the other person will be dissatisfied at ending the conversation at the 'No'. This is particularly so when the 'No' is based on *not able to* rather than *not wanting to*. In such situations you or the other person will want to continue the conversation until an acceptable outcome is achieved. Negotiating is your means of achieving this.

Before going into more detail on this we would like to examine what is going on in terms of needs in such situations.

Conflicting needs

Let's suppose your deputy asks you if he can take his holidays during the last two weeks in August. You have already fixed up yours at this time and you do not think it is desirable for you both to be away at the same time. Your needs and his are in conflict and on the surface it seems that one person's needs can only be met at the expense of the others:

Ways of handling conflicting needs

In the above example you and your deputy could have any of the following behavioural exchanges:

$$agg \longleftrightarrow agg$$
$$agg \longleftrightarrow na$$
$$na \longleftrightarrow na$$
$$ass \longleftrightarrow ass$$

We will look at each of these in more detail.

AGGRESSIVE–AGGRESSIVE EXCHANGE

This arises because each person sees the situation as 'I win/you lose'. In other words, each believes that the only way he or she can win is if the other person loses. Because *both* people believe this, the exchange can be lengthy and draining. A very high proportion of them end in stalemate with no solutions

124

agreed to cope with the conflicting needs. Even where solutions are agreed, there is little chance they will be high-quality, and they will be of the win/lose variety. This is not surprising, because much of the energy of the people involved in such exchanges goes into *beating the other person as opposed to beating the problem*. As we put it in Chapter 8, the *content* gets lost and the *behaviour* takes over.

An underlying theme to many of these interactions is the refusal of one or both parties to accept the needs of the other as legitimate. We will explore this issue in greater depth later.

AGGRESSIVE–NONASSERTIVE EXCHANGE

Our example above could easily fall into this category. You as the manager see your needs as more important than your deputy's, because you are higher in the organization. Your deputy may support this view because he is keen to please. Because of this, there would be no need for you to use heavy aggression, you could just make a rather dismissive statement, e.g. 'I'd be happy for you to take your holidays then, but that's when I'm taking mine and obviously we can't both be away at the same time.' If this is the end of the conversation, then no energy has gone into seeing if there is a way of meeting both sets of needs.

Interactions of this sort often result in solutions that are mundane and low-quality. They are again of the win/lose variety. They have the advantage of being shorter than agg–agg or na–na ones. At the time they may appear satisfactory but later on they often come unstuck. This is because the person being nonassertive has held back on their doubts or disagreements and denied their needs at the time. As we have seen this can lead to resentment and possibly aggression later on.

NONASSERTIVE–NONASSERTIVE EXCHANGE

We see this as a less common exchange in a work environment, but by no means unknown among colleagues and others on the same level within an organization. It is quite common in social life, in situations where people are keen to avoid unpleasantness and to please each other.

Strangely enough, na–na exchanges are similar to agg–agg ones in three ways. They tend to be long, drawn out affairs; they frequently end in stalemate; and the quality of any solutions is likely to be low. This is because each views the situation as 'I lose/you win'. This is to say, each person is wanting the other person to win; each believes that they have to lose in order for the other person to win. When *both* parties are operating from this basis the outcome is often what we refer to as a 'lose/lose', in that the solutions meet *neither set of needs*. They are arrived at by judging them against the criteria of how much they inconvenience, upset, or please the other person. So na–na exchanges are characterized by phrases like:

- 'That wouldn't be fair on you'
- 'No I couldn't let you do that'
- 'That will mean you having to ... You can't possibly do that'

We believe that these exchanges are the ones that lead to win/win outcomes. This means that they meet both sets of needs to an extent that is acceptable to both persons. In some cases both person's needs are met completely. In other cases, they are met to the extent that both persons can walk away from the exchange feeling OK about it. This is not to be confused with a 'compromise' that leaves both parties feeling unhappy about the outcome.

Assertive–assertive exchanges may take a bit longer, because you are searching for outcomes that meet both sets of needs. However, it is this kind of exchange that forms the basis for negotiating acceptable outcomes.

Negotiating acceptable outcomes

You are more likely to negotiate acceptable outcomes of the win/win variety if you *believe* that:

- Your needs are as important as the other person's
- You do not necessarily have to lose for others to win

So it is important to move into negotiating when:

- Someone says 'No' to you and you feel that insufficient time has been given to exploring alternatives
- You are not able to agree to a request from someone and you are not happy to end the conversation at that point

Three useful steps in negotiating are:

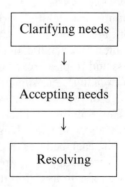

Before going into more detail on each of these steps, you may find it helpful to have an example of a win/win outcome for the situation about the clash of holidays that we described above. One that has been negotiated by a participant after one of our training courses is that he, as the manager, agreed with his deputy that:

1. His two weeks would remain the same, as the holiday was already booked and the deposit paid.
2. The deputy brought his fortnight's holiday forward one week.
3. The deputy agreed to be on call if needed, for the second week when they were both absent.
4. A meeting to allocate and plan the work was arranged on the last day that the manager and his deputy were at work together.

Suggestion 2 was acceptable to the deputy as it still fitted in with his need to have a two-week break with his family. Suggestion 3 was acceptable to the deputy as he was planning some DIY on the house. It was acceptable to the manager as he felt it met his need for sufficient cover. Suggestion 4 made both of them feel more comfortable. The deputy felt it reduced the number of calls he was likely to get at home and the manager felt more confident that the work flow would be maintained.

It is important to stress that this outcome was acceptable to both persons in this situation given the needs they had. The outcome would not necessarily be acceptable to other people in such a situation as their needs could be different. So let us now look at the first steps we describe above.

CLARIFYING NEEDS

The first thing to say is that people do not always talk in terms of their needs. Instead they often put forward suggestions to meet their needs. So you might say to a colleague 'Jane, can we sort out that design problem now rather than this afternoon?' Your unstated need is to be away early tonight to meet a friend at the airport who is arriving from abroad.

Jane does not know this and will probably respond to your suggestion about sorting out the design problem this morning. Fine if it fits in with her needs. However, if it does not she will disagree with your suggestion. When this happens, you may push harder for your suggestion, by for instance pointing out some benefits. However, suggestions are made as a way of meeting needs. In turn reactions, in terms of agreeing or disagreeing, are statements about whether a suggestion meets the other person's needs. So rather than sticking at the suggestion and reacting level, it is often more effective to dig below them and get at the needs. To do this you can:

1. Ask questions to find out from the other person what their needs are. You may need to deal with excuses, hassle, and real reasons before you get to needs. Questions like the following can help you:
'What's the problem?'

127

'How do you mean?'
'How much time do you need to ...?'
'Why is that?'
You may need to ask further questions to follow up the clues about needs that people present. In asking these questions it is important to maintain assertive nonverbal behaviours, otherwise you may be seen as interrogating or negative.

2. State your own needs.
   In the above example, after making your suggestions to Jane, you could simply add your need onto the end. 'Jane, can we sort out the design problem now rather than this afternoon, as I need to be away early this evening?'

You may wish to briefly expand upon your need and why it is important to you. After having done this, get quickly into asking questions to clarify the other person's need.

The needs that emerge will come in all shapes and sizes. Some examples could be:

- 'I need to finish my present survey before taking on another one'
- 'I need to feel confident that any new scheme is going to be an improvement, before I give it the go-ahead'
- 'I need my manager's agreement before I can commit to that and he's firmly against that sort of approach'
- 'I need to get my budget down to target before agreeing on new expenditures'

In some cases, people will not 'come clean' about what their needs really are. This is particularly true where these needs are of a personal nature. If, after listening carefully and asking questions, it leaves you feeling that someone is still holding back you can share your unease by saying such things as:

- 'I sense there may be some other reason why you're not keen to go ahead'
- 'I'm still not clear, Mark, why ...'

If this still does not work, you may be able to deduce or guess what the need may be from the clues that have been put up. The other person's behaviour is making it more difficult to achieve a win/win, but not impossible. So onto the next step.

ACCEPTING NEEDS
Once you are clear on the needs in the situation it is helpful to show the other person explicitly, that you accept their needs as valid. You can empathize and say something like:

- 'OK, Jill, I accept that it is important for you to ...'

or

- 'I recognize your need to . . .'

In turn you want the other person to accept your needs as valid. So you can ask them e.g. 'So do you accept that I need to . . .?'

This may seem a bit unnecessary to you. However, where there is a conflict of needs, it helps you both to focus upon the issue of how to meet both sets of needs. This is in contrast to one person trying to persuade the other that he or she does not 'really' have the need.

RESOLVING

This can be a creative and rewarding exchange, once the needs are accepted on both sides. Listed below are some behaviours that help to create win/win's.

Offer alternative suggestions

These can be new suggestions or they can be variations on ones that have cropped up earlier in the conversation. These variations can be in terms of time, quality, quantity, people. For example, if you cannot let someone have the accurate breakdown of expenditure within the timescale they require, you may be able to let them have an approximate breakdown. This may be sufficient to meet the other person's need, whilst being acceptable to you and hence creating the win/win.

Ask for alternative suggestions

You can share the load of coming up with suggestions with the other person. Given that they have accepted the validity of your needs, they may be as likely as you to come up with the suggestion that leads to or results in the win/win. So questions like the following can help:

- 'How can we get around this one?'
- 'Any suggestions for how we could . . .?'
- 'I'm open to ideas on how . . .'

Strike a bargain

Sometimes it is appropriate to suggest that you will do certain things if the other person will do likewise, for example 'I'm prepared to give a couple of man days to investigating the problem if you will do the same.'

NOTES ABOUT THIS APPROACH

The above approach can result in us achieving more win/win outcomes from situations where there are conflicting needs. You can sometimes get into resolving without explicitly going through the clarifying and accepting needs phase. For instance, someone may make a request of you that you cannot meet. However, you may quickly suggest an alternative way forward that satisfies both of you. It is when your alternative suggestion is not acceptable to the other person that it is worth while taking time out to clarify the needs. Otherwise you can spend time making other suggestions that are not acceptable to the other person. It is quicker and more effective to know the needs and then make suggestions.

In the resolving phase you can find that the other person's suggestions appear to be directed towards meeting their needs and not yours. If this happens, it helps to hold off on making suggestions for a moment and check out whether the other person really does accept the importance of your needs.

Summary

We believe an assertive/assertive exchange gives the best chance of achieving win/win outcomes in situations where there are conflicting needs. Most situations have win/win outcomes, if the people involved are prepared to give some time to identifying them, having accepted the validity of each other's needs.

All situations have win/win outcomes if we consider them in terms of the behaviour rather than just the content. Even if you do not get your needs met, if you have spoken up, made your needs clear and behaved assertively, then you can walk away from the situation feeling good about yourself. Maintaining and enhancing your own self-esteem is the ultimate 'win'!

12. Contributing assertively to meetings

To many managers, meetings are an important part of their job—not only in terms of the time they spend in them, but also because other managers make judgements upon their competence based upon their performance in meetings. You may share this view of the importance of meetings. But do you sometimes have doubts about the effectiveness of meetings, or about your own performance in them? If so, we think you will find this chapter interesting because it aims to help you become more effective in contributing to meetings.

We will concentrate on *contributing to*, rather than *running meetings* because this is the aspect that involves most people. Even when the chairperson is not that skilled at running meetings, by improving your own effectiveness you can do a great deal to make sure the meeting is still effective. In addition, you will be able to adapt some of the items we mention for when you are running a meeting.

Before we go any further, let us say what we mean by a meeting. We are defining a meeting as: *when three or more people come together for at least 30 minutes to achieve a result.*

Now, the success of any meeting depends upon two major factors. For convenience we shall call them the *mechanics* and the *behaviour*. By 'mechanics' we mean such things as:

- The presence or absence of a clear objective for the meeting
- The quality of the agenda
- Whether the 'right' people are there
- Administration—members getting adequate notice, preparation and distribution of paperwork, suitable surroundings, seating arrangements, etc

By 'behaviour' we are referring to what people say and do before and during the meeting. *Both* factors need to be handled well if the meeting is to be successful, but because this book is about behaviour, this is the area we will look at.

We believe any meeting would benefit from more assertive behaviour from both its members and its chairperson. It seems that many people find it more difficult to behave assertively in meetings than they do say in a one-to-one interaction. For instance, you may put forward your ideas, and agree or disagree, when you are interacting with just one other person; yet, in a

131

meeting with six or seven others, you may hold back from stating your ideas, or opinion—behaving nonassertively. On the other hand, you may behave aggressively by overstating your disagreement so that it becomes an attack upon the other person.

This increase in nonassertion and aggression occurs because most people see meetings as more uncomfortable, stressful, or challenging situations than one-to-one interactions. Therefore, they have more faulty inner dialogues and are unclear on the rights they have as members. We will look at each of these in turn, and then we will give some hints for behaving more assertively in meetings.

Inner dialogues for contributing to meetings

If you believe the 'spotlight' is on you when you contribute to a meeting, then you can have some faulty dialogues before, during and after a meeting. Table 12.1 gives examples of some of the sound and faulty dialogues we have

Table 12.1   Examples of inner dialogues about meetings

Faulty inner dialogues	*Equivalent sound dialogues*
Before a meeting	
1. I'm obviously going to be in a minority, so what is the point in saying anything?	I may be in a minority, but I can put over my views concisely and clearly to influence them. If I fail I'll be disappointed, but I'll have done as much as I can.
2. I'll use the meeting to really put Mike on the spot by asking him about the new procedure.	If I'm angry with Mike about the new procedure, then I can raise it with him on a one-to-one without resorting to playing games at the meeting.
During a meeting	
3. If I make my suggestion, other members may think it's silly and I'll look a fool.	I have the right to put forward my suggestion. They may not agree with it but that doesn't mean they'll think it's silly.
4. I can't let Sue get away with that remark, not with all these people here.	I can respond assertively to the remark Sue's just made by asking her what she means by it. I don't need to put her down in front of others.
5. If I ask a question when I don't understand, I'll slow the meeting down and they may think I'm thick.	I can't contribute effectively if I don't understand. So I have the right to ask for clarification. It doesn't mean I'm thick.
6. If I change my mind now I'll lose face and appear to be weak. I can't have that.	I can change my mind, if I want to. It can be a sign of strength rather than weakness.

come across. Take a look at your own inner dialogue, and turn any faulty ones into sound ones. Then you need to be clear about your rights as a member of a meeting, and to accept these rights.

Your rights as a member of a meeting

Most members are clear that the *chairperson* of a meeting has certain rights: for example, the right to interrupt a member who is going on at great length. Also, members are usually fairly clear what these rights are, and they are prepared to give the chairperson these rights in order for the meeting to progress. However, they are often less clear on their *own* rights as a member of a meeting. We cannot be definitive about your rights in the meetings you attend. However, the clearer you are on your rights, and the more you accept them, the more likely it is you will behave assertively in meetings. In the following we suggest some rights that you might have as a member of a meeting. You can decide which ones you believe you have, or would like to have, and can work at accepting them. You may of course need to modify them in the light of your own experience.

We suggest you may have the right to:

- State your opinions and put forward suggestions
- Have these opinions and suggestions listened to and reacted to
- Understand what is being said
- Attend only those meetings, or parts of a meeting, that are relevant to you
- Spend your time productively in meetings
- Disagree with views and suggestions put forward by others
- Make your contributions without being interrupted by others
- Have minutes (where appropriate) that are an accurate reflection of what was said at the meeting
- Know in advance what the objective of the meeting is
- Know in advance roughly how long the meeting will last

As with all rights, accepting or failing to accept the above rights will affect your behaviour. For instance, if you do not accept the right about attending only meetings or parts of a meeting relevant to you, then you will find yourself sitting through all the items of an agenda when only two of them are relevant to you. While this is happening you are probably wanting to be getting on with some other work. Your earlier nonassertion will result in your now feeling restless and frustrated, until you start behaving aggressively, say, with a sarcastic comment about how long it takes the meeting to reach decisions. Accepting the right, on the other hand, encourages you to look for ways of attending just those parts relevant to you. Perhaps you can get the items on the agenda reordered so that you can leave the meeting when your items are over. This way you can reduce the amount of time you spend in meetings where you have nothing to contribute.

So having sound inner dialogues and accepting your rights moves you part way towards being more effective in meetings. In the next section we give some hints that can help you further.

Hints for contributing assertively to meetings

The hints that follow are aimed at helping you to be more influential by achieving a balance between your rights and your responsibilities as a member of a meeting. Some possible rights we listed above.

The general responsibility we believe you have is to make your contributions in ways which help rather than hinder the effectiveness of the meeting. The hints deal with two aspects:

1. Specific behaviours
2. Wider considerations.

SPECIFIC BEHAVIOURS

Stating your views
Use 'I' statements to distinguish opinion from fact and to emphasize they are *your* views, based on *your* experience: 'As I see it, the problem is ...'; 'I find that it works very well.'; 'I believe we do need to tackle this.'; 'My experience is ...'

Agreeing with other people's views and suggestions
It is helpful to others, including the chairperson, if you make your support explicit and concise. So, rather than keeping quiet or nodding your head, actually say you agree. This helps to ensure that useful suggestions are considered rather than ignored by the meeting.

Disagreeing and stating doubts
It is important to say where you stand, including when you do not agree, or when you have any significant doubts. However, these behaviours can easily stop meetings from progressing so it is important to accept the responsibility which goes with exercising the right. This means you need to be constructive:

- Following a disagreement or doubt with a suggestion. 'I do have a doubt, in that ..., so how about ...'
- Keep the disagreement in proportion, by saying what you agree with as well as what you specifically disagree with. 'I agree with your overall approach, Val. However, the part I don't like is ...'
- Give a reason for your disagreement or doubt
- Use phrases like, 'I see it differently', 'My experience is different in that ...'

134

Putting forward suggestions
Suggestions or proposals are statements of *action*. People are more likely to react to them in that way if they *perceive* them as suggestions. So it helps if you can signal a suggestion to the listener by starting it with one of the following phrases: 'How about ...?', 'Shall we ...?', 'I suggest/propose we ...', 'I'd like (us) to ...'.

Asking for clarification
Before reacting to other people's views or suggestions, you may need to check exactly what they mean. Don't put yourself down—'Maybe it's just me, but I haven't understood'. Nor the other person—'You haven't made that at all clear.' Use responsive assertions: 'Pat, when you say the project, do you mean x or y?', 'Have I got this right, you want to ...?', 'What do you mean, Bill?'

Interruptions
By interruptions we mean speaking before someone else has finished. It is denying the other person a fair hearing, so avoid interrupting others to make your point. There are a *few* exceptions to this, for instance where someone has misinterpreted what you said and is pursuing this at length. At this point you need to *signal* your interruption 'Before you go any further, Leslie, let me come in to ...'.

Stave off interruptions from others: 'I'd like just to finish what I'm saying ...', 'Let me just finish ...'.

Asking for reactions from others
People don't always make their position, views and ideas known. So you can encourage them to do so by asking assertively: 'What do you think of my suggestion?', 'What's your view of ...?', 'What ideas do you have for ...?'.

WIDER CONSIDERATIONS

Timing your contributions
If you want to influence a meeting, it isn't just *what* you say and *how*, but also *when* you say it. So:

● Make your contributions at the relevant time—not after an issue has been closed
● If you disagree, make it clear early, rather than waiting until the last minute. Otherwise you could be violating the rights of other members who may become irritated 'Why didn't you say that earlier?'

Not falling in with an 'apparent' majority
Having heard the first two people support a proposal, you may be tempted to hold back on a doubt you have about it. A valid point about the feasibility of

that proposal may then be lost. In addition other members may also keep quiet about their doubts. As a result a proposal with only minimal support gets accepted at the meeting. To prevent this domination of a meeting by a small number of people, who *appear* to be a majority, you need to accept your responsibility to make your doubts and disagreements known.

Deciding which issues to be assertive on and how far to go

If, in a particular meeting, you find yourself out of line with the majority of views being expressed, there may be many issues on which you could take an assertive stand. There is a danger that, if you take a stand on *every* such issue, it will become counter-productive. Other members will start labelling you in their own minds as 'awkward' or 'negative'. In turn, this may colour their opinion of your *views* and so the validity of your points may be lost. To avoid this happening you may have to *decide the crucial issues* on which to stand firm or to speak out.

At other times you may find yourself in the position where, if you were to pursue one particular issue any further, the meeting would be in danger of not achieving its objective. This is probably a good point at which to accept your responsibility and take the initiative for resolving the difference:

- State what *would* be acceptable to you
- Develop other people's suggestions by modifying them or adding two together
- Ask for suggestions for getting around the disagreement

If this fails, as long as you've had a fair hearing, you may decide to let go and go along with the majority. If so, state your position honestly, for example, 'I don't accept . . ., however, in view of the time, I'm prepared to go along with . . .'.

Helping the meeting along

Chairing a meeting is a complex task. We believe that, as a member, you have the *right* and the *responsibility* to help the meeting along. The following are examples of some of the things you can do:

- Suggest that a flip chart or blackboard is used to capture ideas
- Ask for five minutes to study any pages of information you have just been given
- Ask for or make a summary when you feel the meeting is getting 'bogged down'

The following phrases help in making this kind of suggestion more accept-able to the chairperson, while still maintaining your assertiveness. 'Dave, would it be useful if . . .?', 'I'd find it helpful if we . . .'.

136

Getting your fair share of 'air-time'

This is often much more of an issue in meetings that one-to-one conversations. What constitutes a fair share is going to depend upon both the type of and the objective of the meeting. If you are attending a briefing meeting then you would expect enough time to ask questions to check you have understood the information being conveyed to you. You would not expect as much air-time as the person giving the briefing. On the other hand, if you are attending a departmental meeting called to get everyone's reaction to proposed changes, then you would expect to have approximately the same air-time as your colleagues.

Having a degree of clarity about this issue (it's not a science by any means) before you go into a meeting can help you avoid the worst excesses of hogging too much air-time yourself or allowing others to do so.

NOTE ON NONVERBAL BEHAVIOUR IN MEETINGS

In a meeting of seven people there are seven alternative sources of views, ideas and suggestions. To other people you represent just one of the sources. If you are to influence others, it will be by a mixture of what you say and your nonverbal behaviour in saying it. Research suggests that the latter is more important than the former. So if you are to use your air-time effectively, you may need to 'do more nonverbally' than you would during one-to-one conversations. For example:

- Speaking more loudly. The appropriate volume is going to depend on the size of the meeting. If you speak too quietly people may interrupt you or after a while cease to make the effort required to hear you. You may also have difficulty getting in. Raising your voice can help you to get in and have your share of air-time
- Having more eye contact. Who to look at when speaking in a meeting can be a problem. When you are wanting to get in and contribute it can be useful to catch the chairperson's eye or that of the person speaking

  When you are making a point that is relevant to all members, then share your eye contact around. When the point is pertinent to, say two people, then look at them. If you are referring back to what someone has said, then look at that person. Likewise when you are disagreeing with someone. Establishing eye contact helps your voice in that it is directed toward someone, rather than towards the notes on the pad in front of you.
- Using more above-the-table hand actions to help give 'movement' to what you are saying. This increases the chances that you catch other people's attention so that they hear what you say
- Making more use of the space around you. You can add body movements to your hand movements. So steady movements between sitting forward and sitting back in your chair help to signal to others that you are there and involved

Summary

Meetings can, we believe, benefit from increased assertiveness from members and chairpersons. You can make a start on this process for yourself in the next meeting you attend. First of all, check that your inner dialogue is sound; then pick out two or three of the above hints that will be most useful to you initially, and concentrate on these.

If you behaved nonassertively at times in meetings, then you may decide to exercise only certain of your rights and responsibilities initially. For instance, you might start with short, low-risk contributions like making your agreement more explicit, or asking for clarification. Once you have started the process of making more contributions, then you will feel more confident later on to exercise other rights and responsibilities.

If you sometimes behave aggressively in meetings, you could make a start at being more assertive, say, by making your disagreements assertively and by also stating when you agree with someone.

Making a start in these ways is not going to suddenly make the meetings you attend super-efficient. However, it can begin the process of improving these meetings as behaviour is contagious. More assertion from you can lead to more assertion from others.

Equally, if not more important, your increased assertion can help you leave a meeting feeling good about yourself, saying what you had to say and having influenced the outcome of the meeting in some way.

13. Assertiveness and stress

So far in this book we have been making the case that you can be more effective in your job by handling a wide range of specific situations more effectively. We would now like to broaden the approach in the next two chapters and illustrate how assertiveness can help you handle stress and change, two things that are for many people interrelated. We will first look at stress.

Have you ever stepped out into a street and suddenly noticed a car approaching? Instantly your body prepares for action. Your senses sharpen, hormones flood into your bloodstream, your muscles tense, you breathe deeper, your heart rate soars and you feel afraid. You are ready for action and you jump back to the pavement as quickly as you can. After a brisk walk back to work your body sensations return to normal.

At your desk the phone rings. You answer and it is your manager who is not pleased with a proposal you have written and suggests that a lot more work needs to be done on it. You react much as you did in the street half an hour ago. And this time you are left with a sinking feeling in your stomach.

What we mean by stress

Both these incidents led to a stress reaction. *Stress is a normal human reaction to situations and circumstances that we believe hold some threat for us or that we believe we cannot cope with successfully.* In such situations the primitive stress reaction described above, which prepares us to fight or flee, is automatic. When we are able, literally, to fight or flee, the 'energy' released by the stress reaction is used up in the resulting physical activity.

In complex psychological situations however, the problems we face are mental rather than physical and speed of reaction is often not important. In such situations the stress reaction is not just useless but actually harmful. Your body is prepared for physical activity but you are not going to rush upstairs and assault your manager. The energy and tenseness are not readily discharged as you sit and fume about how unreasonable your manager is being. Such frequent surges of stress hormones prime your body to run from things that you cannot escape and the cumulative effect is harmful to both your physical and mental health. It is the frequency and strength of the stress reaction that is the problem. A small amount of stress will put you on your toes for that important meeting or presentation, and you would not be human if you did not sense it from time to time.

To deal with stress we need to be able to recognize the signs. Many of these are internal so it is not always easy to recognize stress in others. The many signs and symptoms of stress are listed in the next section.

The signs of stress

There are two main clusters of reactions that we can have to continued stress and since they feel different it is worth listing them separately. The causation may also be different.

Anxiety is that worried, uptight feeling that something bad or unpleasant is going to happen, or that you are not going to cope effectively.

Depression is that sad and blue feeling that is often associated with disappointment or frustration.

Some anxiety is natural—if you are about to have a very important interview it would be odd if you did not feel anxious. And again some depression is normal—if you fail that interview you are likely to feel depressed or fed up. It is the persistence of these feelings that becomes destructive and affects our ability to get on with life.

Table 13.1 sets out the signs of stress associated with anxiety and depression. It also distinguishes between internal signs and those that other people might notice in you—or you might notice in others.

Some of the above signs most of us will have experienced at one time or another. Taken in isolation any sign is not likely to be a problem; it is when the signs persist or multiply that you may have to do something about it. It is important to note that the physical symptoms listed at the bottom may have other causes and will often need medical attention. Almost any illness may have a stress component and treatment may be affected by stressful circumstances.

The causes of stress

You and a colleague are asked to present next year's departmental business plan at the board meeting next week. You think 'I've never done this before; I'm hopeless at this sort of thing' and distressing anxiety symptoms start. Your colleague thinks 'Great, just the chance I want to put my ideas across' and a not unpleasant tingle of anxiety sweeps from head to toe. When we get down to particular situations stress is very much a unique, individual response.

Like stress itself, the causes of stress are not widely recognized. Stress is not necessarily caused by hard work under pressure; if it were most of our political and business leaders would be cracking up. On the contrary, many of them seem to thrive on it. Stress occurs at all levels in society; indeed it is, if anything, more prevalent in lower status jobs than in the world of the executive. Nor does stress increase with age. The causes can be very

140

Table 13.1 Signs of stress

	Anxiety type	Depression type
Private and internal	poor concentration nervousness, agitation, trembling pounding heart increased eating, smoking, drinking inability to relax loss of sleep troubled breathing sweating increased blood pressure indigestion dizziness	weariness poor concentration and memory boredom, restlessness lack of interest in food, sex, work, life in general feelings of rejection, worthlessness loss of sleep pessimism and despondency resentment, jealousy increased drinking use of anti-depressant drugs
Public and external	easily distracted fussing about details indecisiveness tunnel vision blaming indiscriminately regular aggression taking lots of work home bad driving over-talkative contradictory behaviour marital troubles unable to relax or let go poor delegation bad time management	inertia mood swings social withdrawal apathy indecisiveness suspicion lying, making excuses absenteeism slow response lack of enthusiasm or humour low productivity nonassertive behaviour grumbles and moans avoidance of issues
Other physical symptoms	allergies, diabetes, headaches, backache, ulcers, skin conditions, recurring illness, heart trouble, chest pains	

personal—which is *not* the same as *trivial*—and can occur in any area of your life. Table 13.2 lists most of those features of work and personal life that have been found to be associated with stress.

As was the case with the signs of stress, many of us will also have experienced some of these factors at one time or another. It is our skill in coping with them that determines whether or not we perceive them as stressful.

Is there a basic reason why all of these different factors can cause stress? There does seem to be:

Stress will result in any situation if there is a continuing conflict between what you want or would like and what is actually happening to you.

So, for example, where long hours are concerned if you do not actually want to spend much time with your family or in leisure pursuits then long hours may not be stressful to you.

Table 13.2   Factors associated with stress

Causes	Stress factors
The job itself	• work overload, long hours • qualitative overload, complexity • unclear objectives, ambiguity • continuous demands, conflicting demands • rapid change • machine controls pace rather than person • having to do things you don't want to do • jobs at 'interfaces' and 'boundaries' • expected to influence without authority • inadequate resources • responsibility for people • many interruptions • noisy or distracting environment • dealing with awkward, distressing or dangerous situations • having little or no influence on deadlines or pressure: all external to you and uncontrollable • meetings, presentations, negotiations
Relationships	• inconsiderate, incompetent bosses • competition: low collaboration with colleagues • status, power problems • ineffective communication • managing subordinates • discipline issues • people seen as 'awkward'
Career concerns	• security of job • changes in job, skills, organizations • obsolescent or declining skills • under- or over-promotion • redundancy
Organizational culture	• style of management: closed, aggressive, uninterested • ethos of overwork • mismatch between 'culture' as stated and 'culture' as actually exists • unclear organizational goals • takeovers and mergers: major change
Home vs. work issues	• not enough time for family: conflict work/home • dual-working couples: especially with families

142

Table 13.2 *(continued)*

Causes	*Stress factors*
	• conflict with children • changing male/female roles • mobility expected by company • long hours • taking work home
Personal factors	• poor attention to health (diet, fitness etc.) • over- or under-eating • eating while working • drinking too much • significant life events (etc. bereavement, financial problems, divorce, job change) • no outside interests

Why do we let it happen to us?

The key is in the definition above—*conflict*. At any point in time we are confronted by varied demands and pressures (not all externally generated). We have choices to make. We have our own needs and wants; there are the needs and wants of others. We respond, often, more to the needs and wants of others than to our own.

For instance, you are asked to work on a Sunday. Your inner dialogue may go along these lines: 'I've got things arranged, I've worked late three times this week, my family will be upset but if I don't come in what will they think and others have already agreed so I'd better!' So you agree but the internal conflict goes on and you still have to tell the family. You make up a very good reason for them but the net outcome to you is another increment to your cumulating stress level.

BARRIER BELIEFS

To understand why we let ourselves become stressed, we must first examine the *barrier beliefs* that may underlie our unwillingness to say or to do what we really want. The following are some examples:

Beliefs about self

- I'm powerful and thrive on pressure
- Admitting any difficulties is a sign of weakness
- To get approval I need to cooperate
- It's best to avoid situations that are risky

143

Beliefs about others

- Generally they can't be trusted
- It's best not to tell the truth where other people are concerned
- They seem not to have the worries I have
- They are strongly committed to their work

Beliefs about organizations

- The organization (manager) is to be obeyed
- Expressing doubt or resistance will do you no good at all
- If I do a good job for them, then they'll look after me

In fact, any persistent nonassertive or aggressive behaviour can result in stress in yourself and become a source of stress for others, so review the section on barrier beliefs in Chapter 3.

Preparing to manage stress

One other belief should be mentioned: 'I'm not the sort to suffer from stress.' It is the case that some people clearly showing stress symptoms refuse to admit that there is anything wrong. So the first step to managing stress is to admit to yourself that there is a problem. The list in Table 13.2 will help you to decide.

The next step is to try to analyse what it is in your environment or in your thinking that is causing you stress. As well as identifying and tackling the sources of stress it is also important to improve your physical resilience—which we will cover first in our suggestions for stress management.

PHYSICAL RESILIENCE
Improving your health can lessen the impact of stress on the body. We know that minor infections, aches and pains can multiply when we are feeling run down. So to improve your resistance to stress:

- take regular exercise
- stop smoking
- cut down on alcohol and avoid drugs
- eat a balanced diet low in sugar and fats and high in fibre

PSYCHOLOGICAL RESILIENCE
No matter what causes stress, learning to relax properly will lessen the effects. We have to learn how to relax; it is not enough to flop in front of the television. There is a whole range of techniques; books, audio and video tapes are widely available (even in motorway service areas) which will teach you the basics. You may need to seek some advice to find a technique that

will suit you. But whatever technique you decide to use it is *essential* to keep at it: ten to twenty minutes practice once or twice a day for at least eight weeks and regularly thereafter.

Do not expect instant results: too many people give up after a few attempts. Being able to relax completely, like any other skill, has to be learnt.

BRIEF RELAXATION

During each day you will encounter situations that trigger a stress reaction. Instead of tensing up use such situations as *cues to relax*. Learn to stretch your body and limbs and then let them go limp, do this several times and combine it with taking several slow, deep breaths. See the section on Triggers. Deep breathing forms the basis of many of the longer relaxation techniques. As you learn one of these you will find that the short deep breathing exercise will act as a cue for bodily relaxation.

Tackling the sources of stress

Physical and psychological fitness will begin to decrease the amount of stress, whether anxiety or depression, you feel. But you will need now to identify and deal with the specific sources that are affecting you.

BELIEFS

Examine your beliefs about yourself and the job you are doing. Try to identify any barrier beliefs you may hold and tackle them as described in Chapter 3 on page 42 under 'Modifying beliefs'. Some assertive beliefs that will enable you to combat the conflicting demands at the root of the stress are:

- I can make my own decisions about what is best for me
- My own life is more important than any specific job I have or organization that I work in
- My personal and family life are my top priority
- I can work out a balanced approach to work and other aspects of life
- I am human; I have strengths and limitations and can work with these

INNER DIALOGUES

In Chapter 6 we saw how faulty thinking processes affected our feelings and our behaviour. Faulty thinking is directly linked to the amount of stress we perceive in any situation. For example, if we are about to tackle a difficult negotiation our inner dialogue might be:

- 'This is hopeless, what's the use, I suppose I might as well get it over' (nonassertion) or
- 'They're out to get me so I'll strike first and catch them off guard' (aggression)

An assertive dialogue will enable you to handle such situations with more confidence. Sounder dialogues such as:

- 'This will be difficult, but I have a good case. I'll listen and respond to their points.'
- 'I won't assume they're out to get me. They have a point-of-view. I'll try to understand it and clearly outline the alternative as I see it.'

will enable you to manage such situations with less feelings of stress. Where feelings of stress are concerned it is especially important to include your 'worst fears' in reviewing your faulty thinking processes.

PLANNING WORK AND MANAGING TIME

Earlier we mentioned various organizational sources of stress. Poor time management is a major source of stress, and of low performance. However, before you can tackle any particular time problems you need to make sure you are clear about the objectives and priorities of your job. Use your assertive questioning skills to clarify these with your manager and others to whom you give a service. Once you are clear you can plan where to put the emphasis, what to delegate, and what to stop doing.

There are many books and training courses available on time management, which you can use if you feel this is an issue for you. Whichever approach you take to manage your time, it helps firstly to remind yourself of your rights in this area. For example, your right to:

- Work reasonable hours
- To have clear objectives
- To have feedback and support to do your job

In addition to your questioning skills you will need to be prepared to discuss clearly and openly problems you may be having, and to reach agreed plans to deal with these.

Be realistic about what you can achieve and guard against overplanning. Where you anticipate a particularly difficult situation arising you need to give yourself ample time to think it through and to plan for tackling it—postponing or ignoring it will only magnify the stress.

Finally, take a proper break in your working day: eating on the run will not help your stress level. Get out for a short walk, especially if your job is mostly sedentary.

OTHER PEOPLE

Specific people can be a source of stress; for example, a manager who expects too much, a colleague who does not pass on essential information, staff who continually interrupt. There are many ways in which we can create problems for each other. You can practise your assertion with such people by informing them that what they are doing or not doing is causing problems for you, and reaching agreement about what you would like to happen. As we have said assertiveness gives you the opportunity and skills to raise such issues in ways you can feel comfortable about. The sooner you raise such issues, the less stressful you will find it.

TRIGGERS

Small events can easily set off a stress reaction—being caught in a traffic jam, missing a train, engaged numbers, the expectation of your manager that you are *always* available. Identify your stress triggers, write them down and learn to recognize when stress is affecting you. Strange as it may seem you can use these same situations to combat stress.

When you get caught up in a stressful situation use it as a *cue to relax*. When the traffic is making you tense up, do the opposite—stretch your arms and neck, wriggle your toes and feet, smile at someone in the next car. When the phone is engaged yet again take a deep breath and exhale slowly and repeat two or three times. Use your brief relaxation exercise several times a day in any case to build up your resistance to stress.

Positive inner dialogues are valuable in these trigger situations. If you are kept waiting think 'Good, I've got a few more minutes to collect my thoughts and to relax' and use the minutes usefully. Avoid thinking 'Typical—keeping me waiting again—who do they think they are' and working yourself up into a temper. Think how unproductive it is to let minor daily hassles make you uptight.

LEISURE

For someone under pressure even leisure time can be unsettling. Inability to relax, working long hours, reluctance to take all your holidays, are stress signs. Paradoxically, you need to plan for leisure. Simply lying about in your time off may not be enough. Decide what you like to do in your spare time and make specific plans to do it—theatre seats do not book themselves!

Handling stress in others

Identifying stress in others will not always be easy. The list in Table 13.1 will help but signs can be concealed and, in any case, many of them are internal.

In general it is more helpful to watch out for patterns and trends, rather than take any reaction in isolation, as evidence of stress. Such patterns might be recurring outbursts, declining performance, withdrawal, missed deadlines, short absences. The words, phrases and nonverbal behaviours associated with nonassertion and aggression, if they are becoming frequent, may be indicators of underlying anxiety or depression. Rapid speech, interruptions, talkativeness, fidgeting, outbursts of irritation are typical of anxiety

147

whereas mumbling, lowered interaction, loss of interest, slower movements, and poor posture are more typical of the depressive pattern.

ANALYSIS OF THE PROBLEM

Before you take any active steps you need to analyse the situation under which the person is working. Use the list in Table 13.2 to help you. Observe when and in what circumstances the reactions occur. The causes may lie in work-related factors such as unclear objectives, overload or inadequate training or in career or personal problems.

ACTION

Where a problem is work-related, action may be easily taken. For example, clarification of tasks and outputs, or training in a particular skill may be all that is necessary. Where the stress seems to be related to career or personal concerns a counselling approach is needed.

Whatever the origin, the following guidelines can help with the difficulties of having a productive discussion with the other person.

- Set time aside, and if appropriate arrange time and place
- Start by using 'I' statements to show that you are concerned about aspects of the person's behaviour, e.g. 'Mike I am concerned about ... '
- Try to be specific and indicate what you have noticed and how it is affecting the work
- Use responsive assertion to get the person talking about how they see it and what the reasons may be
- Listen and avoid rushing in with advice or solutions
- Agree that there is a difficulty
- Move on to possible action, again seeking suggestions rather than prescribing action

You may sense that the difficulties are greater than you anticipated and, in this case, you may need to seek advice or suggest that counselling is needed.

This is a difficult and sensitive area. The temptation to leave people alone to sort themselves out is strong. If you do it may become too late to help and more drastic action such as termination of employment may be necessary. You may find that your first attempt may not be readily welcomed: persevere gently, maintain your assertion and remember you have the right to have effective performance from and good relationships with your working colleagues. On a positive note, where less severe stress is concerned, making time available to listen and to talk through the situation will do a lot to help the person concerned.

CREATING A STRESS-FREE ENVIRONMENT

A stress-free environment may be an impossibility but the way you deal with colleagues and staff can reduce the stress level. How about re-reading at this point the lists of causes of stress and check if your behaviour may be the cause of unnecessary stress in others. Specific things you can do are:

- Use empathy to show that you understand people and their problems
- Use responsive assertion to check that workloads and outputs are seen as realistic
- Give praise to recognize and reward effective performance
- Be visible and readily available for consultation
- Involve people in decisions affecting them. It is one of their rights
- Seek their active cooperation and suggestions
- Acknowledge suggestions and give feedback whenever possible.

Summary

Stress is a fact of life. It is widespread, everybody will feel stressed from time to time and, as we said earlier, a certain level can even enhance performance. If you feel stressed recognize the fact and do not pretend that all is well. Get a sound inner dialogue going, 'I can handle it'. Take action, use the above techniques and you will be able to manage the negative impact of pressure. Focus on what you can do something about and reduce the amount of time you spend on those things you cannot do anything about. If a takeover is in the offing you may not be able to prevent it but you could assess your marketability by investigating other jobs.

If you feel that stress is getting the better of you seek help. As a first step discuss how you feel with someone you can trust to help you to decide what to do. As a manager watch for signs in others: give time to people who work for and with you, and you will lessen the likelihood that you are a source of stress to them. Create an atmosphere of interest, quality, and enthusiasm—in such conditions stress is not likely to flourish.

14. Assertiveness and change

The job is going well; you feel in good form; your last appraisal was excellent. But your company is taken over and within a week you are redundant. Change like this can be shattering and scores high as a stress factor. Yet change is an increasing feature of our lives. All the signs are that the ability to cope with and manage change will be an essential ingredient of business and personal success in the future. Before looking at how assertiveness can help you handle change, we would like to say a bit more about change itself.

Change is here to stay

This is nothing new—it was always true. It is as true of human history as it is of nature as a whole. But as we approach the twenty-first century there is little doubt that the pace of change has accelerated and will continue to do so. It is also true that change is not a continuous, even process: it is discontinuous and does not follow easily identified patterns. The pattern of your career before the takeover looked set; the next promotion was in sight had things gone on as you, and others, expected—the company was not doing badly either!

There is a tendency to see change as stressful and, indeed, at times it is. But consider the alternative: no change. For most of us that would be intolerable—to do the same job, in the same way, in the same place, day after day, year after year. It is not change itself that is the problem; it is how we feel about it that determines whether or not we welcome it. In change lies opportunity and if we wish to take these opportunities and enjoy them then we need to understand better the reasons for, and the processes underlying, change. There is little to be gained from denying change or fighting the inevitable. To cope effectively with change we may need to change some of our cherished beliefs about ourselves and the organizations we work in. We will look at some of these beliefs later in the chapter.

It is often said—almost as a self-evident truth—that people resist change. Yet we all change readily in particular circumstances. We surround ourselves with change—new cars, new televisions, new computers, new holidays, new kitchens and so on. In effect, at any time our lives are in a balance where some forces (whether within us or outside) are pushing for change and others are resisting. In order to handle change we need to analyse these forces and then decide in which direction we wish to head. We shall now look at the conditions under which we accept change.

The acceptance of change

Examples based on televisions or cars may seem trivial but they serve to demonstrate how much change we accept, or make in our lives—we could still have the old car or the black and white television. We seek new jobs, promotion, new companies or new partners—constant change in our lives and our surroundings and a lot of it self-generated. And that seems to be the point. Change is readily accepted if you can see the benefits from it and, better still, if you initiate it yourself.

Change affords opportunities to grow, learn and develop: there is no learning without change. Change refreshes and rejuvenates, and enables you to take new perspectives on your life or work. Whether or not we react positively to change may depend on the beliefs that we hold about ourselves and organizations. Beliefs that will help you to accept change include:

- This is an opportunity to increase my skills and knowledge
- It's only by changing that I will make progress
- Nothing is achieved without some change
- Life would be boring without change
- I'm the sort who looks forward to and welcomes change

You can prepare yourself to accept change more readily by cultivating an attitude of openness and enquiry and by seeking opportunities to make appropriate changes in, for example your work, without waiting to be asked or told. Preparing for change will be examined in a later section.

Resistance to change

We see many examples of resistance to change around us both in business and in other aspects of our lives. Some change is clearly not much liked: modern art and architecture are regularly denounced. The nostalgia industry is growing.

People resist change when they believe, rightly or wrongly, that their current situation is threatened or will be worsened by the change. Such beliefs may stem from their past experience of change, or from the way in which the current changes are being managed, or, most likely, from a combination of the two. Even if the current change is being managed superbly, where there is a previous record of badly-managed change the new changes tend to be treated with suspicion and doubt. Such suspicion is enshrined in such beliefs as:

- They never tell you the whole story
- They wouldn't want to change if there wasn't something wrong
- They're always changing and it never gets any better

And in the recent climate of organizational change beliefs about job security are not without some foundation:

● Change always means fewer jobs
● They'll string you along until the worst is over and then drop you

Such beliefs have been absorbed by most of us and are easily activated in situations of ambiguity or doubt. But as we said before, simply resisting change will not do us much good in today's organizational world. Before we discuss how to handle change assertively we will look at the sequence of reactions that change can cause in individuals.

The personal sequence of change

Change seems to trigger a sequence of reactions and feelings that is, to some extent, predictable. Whether the change is positive or negative, wanted or unwanted, the stages in this sequence are remarkably similar. Imagine that you are suddenly made redundant.

SHOCK
Sudden change can produce shock and immobilization—a feeling of being overwhelmed. This is more likely in the case of negative change. Where change is positive this phase may be missed out entirely—or perhaps represented by a state of euphoria.

DENIAL
During this phase people behave as if nothing had happened or they attempt to restore the status quo. Inner dialogues may go along these lines:
'Things will settle down when they realize it's a mistake.'
'Other people may suffer but I should be OK.'

DEPRESSION AND ANGER
The full realization that the change has happened dawns—you are redundant. Change is happening and only you can do anything about your own future. A feeling of powerlessness may lead to depression and apathy. Anger may also be a feature at this stage—energy and time may be wasted trying to get even with the instigators of change:
'I'll show them it was a mistake.'
Those who become apathetic may also waste time by trying to be too helpful to their managers or employers, perhaps in the hope that the status quo will be restored. For this reason a long gap between the announcement and the effective date of the redundancy, though outwardly attractive, may prevent you getting on with the future.
    Even with positive change this sense of depression may set in—several

weeks into that challenging new job reality hits you, feelings of powerlessness can ensue and you think 'Why did I take this job!'

RELEASE AND LET GO

We need to let go of things that we did in the past. That new job will require new ways of working. Often people have difficulty on promotion because they tend to get involved in things they used to do. We need to say to ourselves, 'Forget the past, let's get on with the future.' People who have been made redundant, or forced to change jobs, have a tendency to relive the past and to explain at length how they did things; another tendency is to go into great detail about how and why their job change occurred. A deliberate effort is needed to curb this sort of discussion as listeners are not usually impressed by it.

STABILIZATION AND GETTING ON WITH IT

During this phase the new is accepted. The new job and the new town become as much part of your life as the old ones were. There will still be a lot to learn but you are prepared to get on with it. At this stage, there may be a tendency to denigrate the past; changes are not completely worked through until you can look back and recognize both the good and the bad of the old situation.

It is important to note that each person's reaction to change is unique and the time taken to reach acceptance is variable, and in some cases is never reached. Also, all transitions involve some measure of stress. Winning the pools can lead to the stress of deciding how to spend the money, as well as that of other people wanting to get their hands on it. Let us now see how we can behave assertively so as to manage change in ourselves, and in others, effectively.

Reacting assertively to change

Let us assume that a sudden and unexpected change has occurred and, at first glance, it seems unwelcome. Imagine that you have a choice between redundancy or moving with the company three hundred miles away. How should you handle this? A first step can be to ask yourself:

WHAT ARE MY AIMS?

You will need to clarify what you want from your career. Is this a chance for change or do you want to stay with your company? What do your family think? To carry out such a rational analysis when you may be feeling shocked or angry is not easy. Work on getting a sound inner dialogue that will help you behave assertively in your discussions with the company.

153

FIND OUT ALL YOU CAN

Maintain your assertion as you seek answers to questions about your future job, the future of the company, and details about the redundancy terms. You have the right to know. Recognize that you will not get the perfect answer to all your questions. It is unrealistic to believe that 'they' will have worked it all out in detail. Change is fluid and interactive. The answers you will get will depend, to some extent, on how you behave. As well as the specific job that is on offer you may also want to ask about other possibilities and to begin to make a few approaches to other employers to assess your marketability.

YOU ARE NUMBER ONE

In change of this sort an ostrich-like attitude can take over. There is a tendency to go on working as if nothing is happening and, indeed, to work even harder and become too helpful to others. We are not suggesting that you opt out right away but do not fall into the trap of believing that time is on your side, or if you work harder than ever then, somehow, things will go better for you.

RESISTANCE

Carefully analyse any feelings of resistance you may have. Seek out a trusted, and independent, listener to hear your concerns. Examine your thinking and challenge faulty dialogues such as 'I'll never change now. I'm too old to do this new job. The family will be very upset and anyway it's bound to be bad for the children's education!'

SEE CHANGE AS OPPORTUNITY

When counselling people who have had to make career changes we have been struck by the number of people who say, 'I wish I'd made the change myself a few years ago, before I had to.' You may not have done so but now here is the chance to develop new skills, to seek a better job, or to live in a new part of the country. Many people look back on forced changes with more favour than they felt at the time. The shock and blow to self-esteem has been replaced by the realization that they have benefited and developed as a result.

So from early on strengthen your sound inner dialogue about change being an opportunity. Taking stock of where you are in both your career and your life can only prove valuable. And there may now be an incentive to do something you had always wanted to do—to change direction in your career or to branch out on your own.

Managing change in others

Whole books are written about the management of change so in this short section we will focus on the skills you will need to use in dealing with people directly affected by the change.

OBJECTIVES

Before talking to people you will need to collect as much information as you can about the changes—the reasons for them, the time-scales involved, the process of change (including scope for participation), and so on. Any doubts you may have need to be talked through before you start talking to others. If you do not agree with the change then you need to decide whether or not to make this explicit. Refer back to the section on 'Giving bad news' in Chapter 4.

EMPATHY

Predicting specific reactions to change is very difficult but a safe point to start at is to assume that the change will not be perceived exactly as you see it. Empathy will help you to go some way to identifying possible reactions— try to think how you would react if you were in the other person's position.

Once you start talking to people you will need to be alert to signs that indicate feelings and thoughts that are at variance with what is actually being said to you. You may well be faced with anger or sullen silence. If you are determined to deal humanely with unwelcome change, time will be needed to enable the person concerned to work through the stages already outlined. We recognize, of course, that much change is foisted on people with little concern about the possible emotional reactions—the phone call to pack up and leave does happen. How you handle such change is an ethical issue and handling change in such a brutal fashion would seem to us to be an aggressive rather than an assertive action.

COMMUNICATION

In general, it is more effective to provide people with ample notice of change, whether favourable or unfavourable. We do recognize that there are situations, such as in mergers, where advance notice may not be given to those concerned.

Ideally, though, those concerned should hear about the changes first and preferably face-to-face rather than by telephone or letter. The rumour-mongers work overtime when change is in the offing and the safest way to head them off is to beat them to it. In addition to timing, the sequence of imparting information is of crucial importance. Managers should not be left out of the chain of communication so that they find out after the shop-floor has already been informed.

HANDLING RESISTANCE

To deal assertively with resistance requires you to acknowledge openly that you recognize the resistance. You will need to restate the aims of, and the reasons for, the changes. Be particularly clear about the scope for revision or modification of the plans. Resistance can be lessened by involving those

155

concerned in methods and timescales so that they can have some influence on what is happening. The change itself may not be negotiable but the methods may be.

Answer questions as honestly and openly as you can. If you do not know the answer, say so. Watch the temptation to make promises, or to buy people off with 'sweeteners' you cannot deliver. Under pressure you may feel tempted to blame others in the hope of deflecting the criticism 'Left to me, I wouldn't have done it this way but you know that lot . . .'. In some cases you may sense, rightly, that the resistance is simply token, but do not be temped to minimize even token resistance as this will only serve to increase its strength.

PARTICIPATION

As we have pointed out people accept change more readily if they are involved in it, and accept it better still if they have recognized the need for change. We have a tendency to err on the side of secrecy and caution where change is concerned. This tendency is related to barrier beliefs such as :
'The less people know the better'
'If they hear too soon they'll develop resistance'
In fact, evidence points the other way. Where people are informed openly and assertively and their cooperation sought, they are more likely to respond in a similar manner. Treating people in a manipulative and dishonest way certainly does not work as it soon becomes obvious that deception is being attempted. In such an atmosphere leaks have a remarkable record of appearing. So make every effort to ensure participation in the process of change.

Preparing for change

Since change is becoming an increasing part of our lives what can we do to prepare for it?

AWARENESS

Cultivate an attitude of inquisitiveness about the company and industry you work in. Take an interest in other departments and the people who work there. Ask questions, read notices and company magazines. When you are asked to do things that you do not understand or do not seem to fit in with your job, check out the reasons.

SKILLS

You are more likely to anticipate and cope with changes if you keep your skills up-to-date in your chosen field. Take the initiative in placing youself on training courses or attending conferences or exhibitions. You may decide to attend a course at a local college or undertake one of the many distance learning programmes that are now available.

LIFESTYLE

Guard against getting into ruts or set patterns. Think about your interests—read new authors, try new styles in clothing, listen to music you do not like, look at paintings you would normally dismiss. Take a different route to work, try a new holiday resort, vary your working day and so on.

Such advice may not seem relevant to helping you handle major change. However, there is evidence that people who have a flexible and optimistic outlook on life, and who are not slaves to routine, are better at handling change whether in themselves or in others.

Unacceptable change

Only you can decide when change is unacceptable. If you find that you are strongly resisting a particular change it may be that it is unacceptable. And if this is the case, the assertive response is to make your concerns known and to seek all the information you can about the proposed change. If you are powerless to influence the change in the way you would like you may be left with no option but to leave the situation. To do otherwise may lead to conflict and stress. You have the right to have your own opinions and beliefs and, in some situations, to deny them leaves you feeling highly dissatisfied.

Summary

Change in organizations tends to have a bad image. It is easy to criticize change, to be cynical about it and to encourage others to do likewise. And not all change is necessary or well thought out, change for changes sake can become almost endemic. New managers before they have had time to get to know their new department, can rush around reorganizing everything. Such change is often not worth resisting. The assertive posture is to keep an open mind, learn from the change and contribute what you can: covert resistance is nonassertive.

Whatever the merits of any particular change, change as we said, is here to stay. It exists all around us in industry and in public life. In change lies the hope of progress. Remember that life itself is based on change and that stability, welcome as it is at times, is only a pause on the journey.

157

15. Continuing to increase your assertiveness

As we have gone along in this book, we have suggested that you take time out from reading to practise some of the things we are talking about. In this last chapter we aim to help you keep your learning going, so that you continue to become more assertive.

As we have said before, although it is not easy, you can change your behaviour if you want to. As the last chapter illustrated, your life to date has consisted of a continual process of change—acquiring various patterns of behaviour, and then adjusting some and discarding others. But so far this process has not always been under your conscious control, so some of the behaviours were acquired in a random way. Because of this it is likely you have some behaviours that in retrospect you now consider to be less productive and rewarding than other behaviours. So the issue is not about whether you can or cannot change, but rather about whether you take control of those changes or not. The point is that you can direct the changes in whatever way you want them to go.

We will assume that you want to change your behaviour in the direction of increasing your assertion! So what can you do to make sure your efforts will lead to increased assertion as opposed to increased aggression or nonassertion? We would like to highlight the following four steps:

- Choosing the right situations
- Preparing for these situations
- Behaving assertively during these situations
- Reviewing situations afterwards

We will give some hints on each of these steps in turn.

Choosing the 'right' situations

Changes in behaviour come in small steps. So choose situations in which you believe *you have a reasonably good chance of maintaining your assertion*. If you choose very difficult situations initially (for instance, standing up to a very aggressive senior manager), then you may be trying to take too big a step. Failure at this stage may lead you into having a faulty dialogue ('I knew it wouldn't work when it came to the crunch') and also to reducing your confidence in your ability to implement what you have learned.

Other factors to consider in selecting situations are the benefits and consequences that can follow from your increased assertion in a situation. So you need to weigh the benefits against the possible negative consequences of standing up for your rights. Ideally, you are looking for situations where the benefits clearly outweigh any negative consequences.

People who have been on our training programme have chosen a wide range of situations to work on when they have returned to work. Below we describe a number of them along with the outcomes, to give you an idea of the sort of situations you can choose to work on initially.

1. Just after returning from the training programme, Simon was asked by his manager to work on a project on the continent. This would involve him spending long periods away from home.

Simon appreciated the opportunity for development that this represented, but was not keen at this particular time on the thought of the periods away. He collected as much information as he could at this initial phase and then asked for time to reflect on the request and to clarify his concerns.

At the subsequent meeting he clearly stated his concerns while stressing his appreciation of the opportunity. His manager agreed to put these concerns to the instigator of the project and to ask for suggestions to overcome them. The outcome was an agreement that Simon felt happy with and represented a win/win for him and the project manager.

Prior to the training, Simon felt he would have readily agreed to go, with no negotiation, even though he would have been unhappy with the periods away from home.

2. Pam, a member of staff, came to Jane saying she wanted to change her job to gain promotion. Jane felt Pam needed to improve her performance in her present job before she could be recommended for promotion. Jane had been a bit dismissive when Pam had raised the issue once before. This time Jane had a lengthy discussion with Pam and uncovered a number of things that Pam was unhappy about. A one-month review plan was agreed. Pam's performance improved over the month, and at the review she stated that she no longer wished to change jobs.

3. At an important presentation of quarterly results to senior managers, William explained the prospects for the future. Normally he would have left it there. However, this time he went on to point out some of the risks, as he saw them, for the future.

After some tough questioning, the director said he had found the new information very useful.

4. Sue was working on a project with a deadline that she felt had become unrealistic, as a result of a number of problems she had encountered. Instead of keeping quiet about her concern she raised it with her manager.

After outlining the problems, she proposed what she thought was a realistic completion date. Further negotiations, involving proposals for changing other priorities, eventually resulted in her manager's agreement to the new completion date.

5. At an annual performance appraisal with his manager, Mike stated that he believed he had effectively addressed the major point of criticism from the previous appraisal. His manager was not convinced. Mike nearly left it at that point. However, he decided to pursue the issue and he went on to assertively outline examples of what he had done differently. His manager then agreed to improve the rating he had given.

Preparing for situations

This is crucial, in our experience. If you can spend a short while before an important situation working through the following steps, then you are more likely to be successful in that situation:

- Getting clear what you want to achieve from the situation (your objective)
- Clarifying your and the other person's rights
- Turning any faulty dialogues into sound ones
- Playing out in your own mind the assertive statements with which you want to start the interaction

Initially, you may want to jot down some notes under each of these headings. Later on you can dispense with notes and just get things clear in your own mind. You can do this as you travel to work or even in the two or three minutes as you walk to the office of the other person involved. You can practise saying to yourself the actual words you will use, along with the appropriate tone of voice. This will help you to start off the interaction on an assertive note. If you start off badly on an aggressive or nonassertive note, it can be difficult to recover.

Also, it can be helpful to work out your responses to some of the predicted 'hassles' that the other person may make. By 'hassles' we mean the statements that people use when they do not accept your assertion. Tables 15.1 and 15.2. which are examples of preparing for situations, include some instances of hassles. We are not necessarily suggesting that you go into this much detail in preparing: we have done so simply to illustrate the approach. Also, we have added a description of the situations to put the examples into context.

Behaving assertively during these situations

Having done some preparation along the lines described, you have a *healthy* degree of confidence in the situation itself. With this sort of confidence you are more likely to behave assertively. If you make your initial assertion as planned, this should get you off to a good start. If the predicted hassles come up, you can also handle them as planned.

160

Table 15.1   Preparation for situations: Example 1

Description of situation
A request for capital expenditure. My manager (Ian) has agreed it, and it now needs to be approved by his manager (Ron). Ron has a lot of other expenditure requests and he is very busy at present. I am due to see him later today, with Ian, to make my case. Ian tends to become nonassertive in this sort of situation.

My objective in this situation
To get Ron to approve my capital expenditure request.

Rights in situation

(a) Mine:	I believe I have the right to:
	• Put my case for the request and have it listened to
	• Expect Ian to make it clear that he is in favour of it
(b) Other person:	I believe Ron has the right to:
	• A clear presentation of the facts, both for and against
	• Make the final decision

Inner dialogue

Faulty dialogue	*Equivalent sound dialogue*
Ron has so many other requests. He's so busy I can't see how I stand a chance of convincing him.	My request is as important as anyone else's, and I believe I can make out a good case for it.
Ian will do his usual trick of keeping his head down and won't support me.	It would be nice to have Ian actively supporting me, but if not I can get Ron's agreement on my own.

My initial assertion
'Ron, about this capital expenditure request of mine: I appreciate that you have a lot of others to deal with. However, I believe there are substantial benefits that will follow from this expenditure.'

Predicted hassles	*Assertive responses*
'They'll need to be substantial; things are really tight at the moment.'	'I do see the benefits as substantial and would like to outline them to you.'
'It sounds all right, but how can you be sure you'll make those savings?'	'The savings I've mentioned are based on a detailed comparison that I've made with last year's figures. I believe they are realistic.'

It is possible that unexpected hassles will come up. The key to handling these is to 'buy yourself some time' in order to get a sound inner dialogue going and to think of an assertive response. You can do this very quickly. When we talk of buying time we are thinking of split seconds or seconds at the most. Here are some ways of 'buying time':

- Weighing of words: 'Well, ...', 'Fine, ...', 'OK, ...', 'I see, ...'
- Responsive assertions, in the form of seeking clarification or testing your understanding: 'Do you mean ...?' or 'Have I got it right, what you're saying is ...?'

- Asking for 'time out': 'I'd like a moment to think about that', or 'Let me see now', or 'Now, let me ponder this'.

Table 15.2   Preparation for situations: Example 2

Description of situation
Jane, one of my staff, is being considered for promotion to section manager. This is a newly created position within my department. She has recently been involved in a couple of tricky situations, which my director (Doug) believes she did not handle very well. Jane has a good record of success over the two years she has been with me, and I believe she should be offered the section manager's job.

My objective in this situation
To get Doug's agreement to offer Jane the section manager's job.

Rights in situation
(a) Mine: I have the right to make up my own mind about Jane and to recommend her for the job.
(b) Other person: Doug has the right to make the final decision on whether Jane is offered the job.

Inner dialogue

Faulty dialogue	*Equivalent sound dialogue*
I know Doug doesn't rate Jane, so if I disagree with his judgement, he'll doubt my judgement.	Just because my judgement is different from Doug's doesn't mean it's wrong.
Doug's biased, and nothing I can say will make him change his mind.	I think that Doug has formed his opinion of Jane on the basis of recent events. I can give him evidence of Jane's good work over the past two years. He may change his mind after this.

My initial assertion
'Doug, before you finally make up your mind about Jane, I'd like to discuss her overall performance with you.'

Predicted hassles	*Assertive responses*
'I think the last couple of weeks have convinced me that she's not the right person for the job.'	'I recognize that Jane did not handle those recent situations well. However, I think they were very tricky ones. I'd like to put that alongside her good performance over the past two years.'
'I just don't think Jane is up to it.'	'What parts of the job do you think Jane will have difficulty with?'

Reviewing situations afterwards

As you walk back to your office or travel home in the evening, you will probably find yourself thinking about the situations you have been involved in. When you are doing this, it is essential to be realistic about both your successes and your failures.

When you are considering your successes, do not down-play them, or exaggerate them. Being honest with yourself about your successes provides you with an objective basis for making progress in the future.

Because you are trying out new or modified approaches in handling situations, you may be unsuccessful in any of the following ways:

- You fail to maintain your assertion
- You do not achieve your objective
- The other person does not accept your right to be assertive

In all these cases you want a sound inner dialogue afterwards, so that you can rationally analyse what happened and learn from it. Faulty dialogues like 'I knew I'd mess it up' will work against your learning from the situation. In contrast, sound dialogues like the following ones help to ensure that you keep on developing your assertive skills:

- 'I wasn't successful in achieving my objective, but I reckon I know why'
- 'Roy responded aggressively, and I think found it difficult to accept that I have the right to suggest alternative approaches. I can clarify this with him next time it happens'

As a result of reviewing your behaviour in this way, you can work out improved responses to the situations that you can predict will occur. You can also start working on other areas of your assertiveness in which you feel you can make improvements. At the same time, you can begin to increase your assertion in some of those more difficult situations that we suggested you avoid tackling early on. So, having got some successes under your belt, you can choose, for instance, to stand up to the very aggressive senior manager that we referred to early on in this chapter. However, before rushing into action on this, we suggest you consider the benefits and consequences and prepare carefully, so that you are clear beforehand on how far you are going to push your assertion.

Handling unexpected situations

Sometimes, of course, you are not able to prepare for situations—for instance, when someone bursts into your office and is aggressive to you about a new policy announcement. It usually helps in such situations if you buy yourself some time in the way we described earlier in this chapter.

In the early days of learning to be more assertive, these situations can be very demanding. It is important, therefore, to be realistic about your performance in these situations. Do not berate yourself afterwards with such statements as 'Why didn't I think of it at the time? What I should have said to him was . . .'.

163

A final few words

A lasting increase in your assertion will come about only if you do keep practising and reviewing. This way, the assertive behaviours we have referred to in the book become an integrated part of your behaviour. Being realistic when you review your performance ensures that you recognize your successes and keep your failures in perspective. It may help you to understand some of these failures if you remember that some people may have a vested interest in your *not* becoming more assertive.

Index